Jim Britt's

Cracking the Rich Code[16]

Inspiring Stories, Insights and Strategies from Top Thought Leaders Around the World

STAY IN TOUCH WITH JIM BRITT

www.JimBritt.com

www.CrackingTheRichCode.com

www.PowerOfLettingGo.com

Cracking the Rich Code[16]

Jim Britt

All Rights Reserved

Copyright 2024

CTRC Publishing and Training, Inc.

10556 Combie Road, Suite 6205

Auburn, CA 95602

The use of any part of this publication, whether reproduced, stored in any retrieval system, or transmitted in any forms or by any means, electronic or otherwise, without the prior written consent of the publisher, is an infringement of copyright law.

Jim Britt

Cracking the Rich Code[16]

ISBN:

Co-authors from Around the World

Jim Britt

Carlos Hoyos

Bonita Palmer

Gayathri Riddhi

Doug Giesler

Max Willett

Dr. Damian Nesser

Luannah Victoria Arana

Jean Yeap

Sharon Hughes

Daniela Man-Romania

Ann Holland

Lynette Weldon

Shafer Stedron, MD

Trisha Fuller

Marla Press

Georgene Summers

Erica Gifford Mills

Bertie Le Roux

Cindy MacCullough

Chase Hughes

DEDICATION

Entrepreneurs will change the world. They always have and they always will.

Dedicated to the entrepreneurial spirit that lives within each of us.
God Bless America and the World!

PREFACE
Jim Britt

In pursuit of a meaningful and fulfilling life, the concept of richness extends far beyond mere financial prosperity. It encompasses a holistic approach, embracing abundance in every facet of our existence—financial, emotional, intellectual, and spiritual. "Cracking the Rich Code with 21 Top Thought Leaders" is not just a manual for accumulating wealth; it is a comprehensive guide to attaining riches in all areas of life.

The journey to holistic riches is a transformative odyssey, and within these pages, you'll find the collective wisdom of 21 experts who have not only achieved remarkable success in their respective field but, have also cracked the code to living a truly rich and fulfilling life, while helping other to do the same. Their stories, insights, and strategies are the keys to unlocking doors to prosperity abundance and well-being.

Our esteemed contributors are visionaries who understand that true richness transcends financial accomplishments. Their perspectives span the spectrum, from business, to personal development, mindfulness, relationships, health and wellness, and spirituality. Each chapter in this book serves as a beacon of guidance, offering a unique perspective on how to navigate the intricate pathways of life to attain richness in all dimensions.

As you delve into the following pages, you'll be introduced to the stories of these remarkable individuals who have not only achieved success in their respective fields, but have also cultivated richness in their relationships, health, and sense of purpose. Their experiences are a testament to the idea that true wealth is a compellation of material prosperity, and the riches found in our connections, personal growth, and the alignment of our actions with our deepest values.

True richness moves beyond the material realm into emotional richness. Emotional intelligence, resilience, and the ability to navigate the complexities of human relationships. Each coauthor offers practical tools and perspectives that will empower you to forge deeper connections, overcome challenges, and find joy in your everyday interactions.

Intellectual richness is also a dimension often overlooked in the pursuit of a rich life. From innovation and creativity to conscious learning and adaptability, intellectual richness is the fuel that propels us forward. All creation begins with an idea. The contributors share their insights into cultivating a curious mind, staying ahead of a rapidly changing world, and leveraging knowledge to create a life of richness and purpose.

Spiritual richness takes center stage too. Beyond religious affiliations, spiritual richness encompasses a profound connection with oneself, others, and the universe. These thought leaders share their journeys of self-discovery, mindfulness, and the pursuit of a higher purpose, offering a more rich and meaningful existence.

This book is not a one-size-fits-all prescription for richness; it a diverse tapestry of ideas, experiences, and strategies that you can tailor to your unique journey. Whether you are an entrepreneur seeking business and financial success, or an individual navigating the complexities of relationships. A lifelong learner, or someone on a spiritual quest, "Cracking the Rich Code" has something for you.

As you embark on this transformative journey with our diverse lineup of thought leaders and experts, just remember that richness is not a destination but a continuous exploration. May the insights and strategies within these pages serve as catalysts for your personal and collective growth, guiding you toward a life of richness in every sense of the word.

Wishing you abundance fulfillment, and richness in all areas of your life.

And remember, just one idea acted upon can change your life. Happy hunting!

Jim Britt

The world's top 50 most influential speakers and top 20 life and success strategist.

www.JimBritt.com

www.CrackingTheRichCode.com

www.PowerOfLettingGo.com

Foreword by Brian Tracy

Life is always a series of transitions... people, places and things that shape who we are as individuals. Often, you never know that the next catalyst for change is just around the corner, in someone you meet, on a page of a book or in a moment of self-reflection.

As the author of 93 books myself, you can imagine how fussy I am to write a foreword to publications in the business and self-development space. My friend Jim Britt is an exception. He has spent decades influencing millions of individuals with his many best-selling books, seminars, programs and coaching, to blossom into the best version of themselves. He has the knowledge, wisdom and skillsets needed to make a significant contribution to overcoming issues entrepreneurs face in business today. His success speaks for itself.

In a world where the pursuit of wealth and success often dominates our collective consciousness, the concept of cracking the rich code has become an elusive quest for many. We marvel at the seemingly effortless success stories of millionaires and billionaires, wondering what secret knowledge or hidden talents they possess that have propelled them to riches. Yet, behind every success story lies a unique and inspiring journey, woven with challenges, triumphs, and invaluable lessons learned.

It is with great excitement that I present to you "Cracking the Rich Code," a book that unveils the remarkable successes of 20 millionaire coauthors. These individuals have not only achieved extraordinary success, but have also generously shared their insights, strategies, and wisdom, inviting the readers to embark on their own transformative journeys.

Within these pages you will discover a variety of stories that defy the myth of an easily attainable overnight success. Instead, you will discover stories of resilience, determination and the unrelenting decisions to pursue their dreams. Each author offers a unique perspective on wealth creation, sharing the secrets they unlocked along their path to financial success.

As you read each chapter you will encounter diverse backgrounds, highlighting the fact that the rich code is not for a certain gender, race, age or social status. You will discover that there are a myriad of ways in which financial success can be achieved.

So, prepare to be inspired as you witness the transformative power of perseverance and the unwavering belief in one's abilities. Through their stories, each coauthor will take you behind the scenes of their successes, allowing you a glimpse into the countless hours of hard work, sacrifices, and failures they encountered along the way.

This book is not just about destination; it's about the journey. Beyond the accumulation of wealth, these authors emphasize the importance of personal growth, finding purpose, and making a positive impact on the world. They share their experience of self-discovery and self-improvement, and offer guidance on developing the mindset, habits, and values necessary to build sustainable success in any and all areas of life.

Their stories will reveal that the rich code is not a hidden secret, but rather a blueprint for anyone willing to embrace the principles with dedication and perseverance. It's about learning from failures, embracing risks, overcoming fears, and continuously expanding one's knowledge and skills. It's about having a mindset of abundance, nurturing relationships, and giving back to society.

Whether you are an aspiring entrepreneur, a seasoned professional, or simply seeking inspiration and guidance, "Cracking the Rich Code" will provide a roadmap to unlocking your real potential. Through the diverse perspectives of Jim Britt and the coauthors, you will find a wealth of actionable strategies, that will empower you to rewrite your own story and chart your course toward financial prosperity.

Let's help in this quest, as Jim Britt and the talented coauthors unselfishly donate their most important asset, their precious

LIFETIME of experience, to elevate one life at a time to their full potential and greatness.

If I were you, I would buy 10, and then giftwrap them to acknowledge your most important top ten relationships in life or clients in business. By doing so, you will strengthen the relationship and encourage others to live a more fulfilling life.

As you close the pages of any of the books in this series, you will gain a new life of clarity and focus as never before. *Cracking the Rich Code* will provide tools to transform results for corporations, institutions, and individuals, both personally and financially.

If you've ever wanted to read a book that challenges you to become more than you are and leaves you with enough inspiration to last a lifetime, *Cracking the Rich Code* is it!

Allow all you have read in this book to create introspection and redirection if required.

Remember, death is certain. Success is not. This life is your journey to craft.

Brian Tracy

Table of Content

Jim Britt vii

Foreword by Brian Tracy xi

Jim Britt 1
   Think Like Superman

Max Willett 13
   Living Maxed Out

Bonita Palmer 25
   The Ripple Effect:Transforming Relationships into Business Success

Carlos Hoyos 35
   From Battling Cancer to Global Executive Coach & Business Advisor: Shaping the Transformational Leadership of the Future

Ann Holland, PhD 47
   Where the Rubber Meets the Road!

Doug Giesler 55
   Unlimit your limit!

Daniela Man 67
   Cellular Reset: Unlocking Your Full Potential for Success

Luannah Victoria Arana 79
   The Power and Possibility of You!

Bertie le Roux 93
   Belief to Achieve:An Entrepreneur's Journey from Invisible to Invincible

Gayathri Riddhi 101
   Mindfully Shift to Winning Mindsets:Transform Your Leadership to Thrive in Uncertainty

Shafer Stedron, MD 113

Pruning: A Neurologist's Guide to Mastering Your Mindset: Begin to Build the Life You Truly Want

Damian Nesser Ed.D. 123

From Struggles to Strength

Jean Yeap: Founder & Visionary Entrepreneur 133

Frustration Led Me to Build a Business The Birth of La gourmet®: Creating High-Quality, Affordable Cookware for Healthy Living

Georgene Summers 147

Fear, the Great Disabler!

Erica Gifford Mills 157

Boundary Management:The Foundation for Personal and Professional Growth

Lynette Weldon 169

The Courage to Live Authentically: A Journey to Purpose and Gratitude

Sharon Hughes 179

Emotional Richness: The Hidden Key To Success

Trisha Fuller 191

Lindsay's Story: A True Story, A Last Resort

Marla Press 203

Create the Richer You

Chase Hughes 213

Your New Butler

Cindy MacCullough 223

When the Rubber Meets the Road

Afterword 237

(this page is intentionally left blank)

Jim Britt

Jim Britt is an award-winning author of 15 best-selling books and ten #1 International best-sellers. Some of his many titles include Rings of Truth, Do This. Get Rich-For Entrepreneurs, Unleashing Your Authentic Power, The Power of Letting Go, Cracking the Rich Code and The Entrepreneur.

Jim is an internationally recognized business and life strategist who is highly sought after as a keynote speaker, both online and live, for all audiences.

As an entrepreneur Jim has launched 28 successful business ventures. He has served as a success strategist to over 300 corporations worldwide and is one of the world's top 50 most influential speakers and top 20 life and business success strategists. He was presented with the "Best of the Best" award out of the top 100 contributors of all time to the Direct Selling industry.

For over four decades Jim has presented seminars throughout the world sharing his success strategies and life enhancing realizations with over 5,000 audiences, totaling almost 2,000,000 people from all walks of life.

Early in his speaking career he was in business with the late Jim Rohn for eight years, where Tony Robbins worked under Jim's direction for his first few years in the speaking business.

As a performance strategist, Jim leverages his skills and experience as one of the leading experts in peak performance, entrepreneurship and personal empowerment to produce stellar results. He is pleased to work with small business entrepreneurs, and anyone seeking to remove the blocks that stop their success in any area of their life.

One of Jim's latest programs "Cracking the Rich Code" focuses on the subconscious programs influencing one's relationship with money and their financial success. www.CrackingTheRichCode.com

Think Like Superman

By Jim Britt

"Waking up to your true greatness in life requires letting go of who you imagine yourself to be."

--- Jim Britt

FACT: Becoming a millionaire is easier than it has ever been.

Many people have the notion that it's an impossible task to become a millionaire. Some say, "It's pure luck." Others say, "You have to be born into a rich family." For others, "You'll have to win the Lotto." And for many, they say, "Your parents have to help you out a lot." That's the language of the poor.

A single mother with five children says, "I want to believe in what you're saying. However, I'm 45 years old and work long hours at two dead-end jobs. I barely earn enough to get by. What should I do?"

Another man said, "Well, if you work for the government, you cannot expect to become a millionaire. After all, you're on a fixed salary and there's little time for anything else. By the time you get home, you've got to play with the kids, eat dinner, and fall asleep watching TV."

Everyone has a story as to why they could never become a millionaire. But for every story, excuse really, there are other stories OR PEOPLE with worse circumstances that have become rich.

The truth is that all of us can become as wealthy as we decide to be, and that's a mindset. None of us is excluded from wealth. If you have the desire to receive money, whatever the amount, you have all of the rights to do so like everyone else. There is no limit to how much you can earn for yourself. The only limitations are what you place on yourself.

Money is like the sun. It does not discriminate. It doesn't say, "I will not give light and warmth to this flower, tree, or person because I don't like them." Like the sun, money is abundantly available to all of us who truly believe that it is for us. No one is excluded.

There are, however, some major differences between rich and poor people. Here are some tips for becoming rich.

Change Your Thinking

You have to see the bigger picture. There are opportunities everywhere! The problem is that most people see just trees when they should be looking at the entire forest. By doing so, you will see that there are opportunities everywhere. The possibilities are endless.

You'll also have to go through plenty of self-discovery before you earn your first million. Knowing the truth about yourself isn't always the easiest task. Sometimes, you'll find that you are your biggest enemy—at least some days.

Learn from Millionaires

Most people are surrounded by what I like to call their "default friends." These friends are acquaintances that we see at the gym, school, work, local happy hour, and other places. We naturally befriend these people because we are all in the same boat financially. However, these people aren't millionaires in most cases and cannot help you become one either. In fact, if you tell them, you will become a millionaire, some may even tell you that it's impossible and discourage you from even trying. They'll tell you that you're living in a fantasy world and why you'll never be able to make it happen. Instead, learn from millionaires. Let go of these relationships that pull you down regarding your money desires. It's okay to have friends that aren't millionaires. However, only take input from those who have accomplished what you want to accomplish. Hang out with those who will encourage and help you reach the next level. Don't give your raw diamonds to a bricklayer to cut.

Indulge in Wealth

To become wealthy, you must learn about wealth. This means that you'll have to put yourself in situations that you've never been in before.

ON OCCASION, DO SOME OF THESE:

Fly first class and see how it makes you feel.

Eat out at the finest restaurant, and don't look at the price on the menu.

Take a limo instead of a cab or Uber. Watch how you feel.

Reserve a suite in a first-class hotel.

If you are used to drinking a $20 bottle of wine, go for the $100 and see how it tastes. It does taste different.

All I am saying is, try some things that wealthy people do and see how it makes you feel.

Believe it is Possible

If you believe it is possible to become a millionaire, you can make it happen. However, if you've excluded yourself from this possibility and think and believe that it's for other people, you'll never become a millionaire.

Also, be sure to bless rich people when you can. Haters of money aren't likely to receive any of it either.

Read books that millionaires have written. By gaining a well-rounded education about earning large sums of money and staying inspired, you'll be able to learn the wealth secrets of the rich. I just saw a video on LinkedIn with my friend Kevin Harrington from the TV show Shark Tank. He said that one of his new companies just had a million-dollar day on Amazon.

Enlarge Your Service

Your material wealth is the sum of your total contribution to society. Your daily mantra should be, *'How do I deliver more value to more people in less time?'* Then, you'll know that you can always increase your quality and quantity of service. Enlarging your service is also about going the extra mile. When it comes to helping others, you must give everything you have. You just plant the seeds, and nature will take care of the rest.

Seize ALL Opportunities That Make Sense

You cannot say "No" to opportunities and expect to become a millionaire. You must seize every opportunity that has your name on it. It may just be an opportunity to connect with an influential person for no reason. Sometimes the monetary reward will not come immediately, but if you keep planting seeds, eventually, you'll grow a fruitful crop. Money is the harvest of the service you provide and sometimes the connections you have. The more seeds you plant, the greater the harvest.

Have an Unstoppable Mindset

Want to know some of what my first mentor shared with me that took me from a broke factory worker, a high school dropout, to a millionaire?

First, he said, you must start thinking like a wealthy, unstoppable person. You must have a wealth mindset. He said that wealthy people think differently. He said, "I want you to start thinking like Superman!" Sounds crazy, right? Well, it's not. It's powerful, and here's why. How you think will change your life.

Wealthy people think differently. They really do. And anyone can learn to think like the wealthy.

I'm not talking about positive thinking, the Law of Attraction, or motivation. Let's get real. None of that stuff works anyway. Otherwise, we would all be prosperous and happy already. Instead, I'm talking about thinking based on quantum physics. Once you understand and apply it, it will change your life. You will become unstoppable!

If there was any fictional or real person whose qualities you could instantly possess, who would that person be? Think about it. Personally, I would say that Superman is the perfect person. Now, you are probably thinking I have lost it, right? Just stick with me here. You will like what you are about to hear.

Superman is a fictional superhero widely considered one of the most famous and popular action heroes and an American cultural icon. I remember watching Superman every Saturday morning when I was a kid. I couldn't get enough. He was my hero!

Let's look at Superman's traits:

Superman is indestructible.

He is a man of steel.

He can stop a locomotive in its tracks.

Bullets bounce off him.

He is faster than a speeding bullet.

No one can bring him down.

He can leap tall buildings in a single bound. Great powers to have in this day and age, wouldn't you say? What else would you need?

Now, for all you females, don't worry. We have not left you out. There is also a female version of Superman named Superwoman. She has the same powers as Superman.

Now, this is where it gets interesting. Let's first look at the qualities that Superman possesses that you want to make your own. And to make it simple, I will refer to Superman for the rest of this message, and you can replace him with Superwoman if you are female.

Again:

Superman is powerful and fearless.

Superman is virtually indestructible—except for kryptonite, of course.

Superman can stop bullets.

Superman has supernatural powers. He can see through walls.

Superman can stop a speeding locomotive.

Superman can stop a bullet.

Superman jumps into immediate action when troubles arise.

Superman can crash through barriers.

Superman can even change clothes in a phone booth in seconds. Not too many of those around anymore. You'll have to duck behind a building to change.

So, you're thinking right now, *'Okay, I know that Superman has incredible supernatural powers, how can that help me? What good will it do me to think I am Superman, a fictional character?'*

Here is where science comes in. This is the part where you will be amazed when you learn about the supernatural powers you already possess! NO, REALLY!

Your brain makes certain chemicals called neuropeptides. These are literally the molecules of emotion, like love, fear, joy, passion, etc. These molecules of emotion are not only contained in your brain but circulate throughout your cellular structure. They send out a signal, a frequency much like a radio station sending out a signal. For example, you tune in to 92.5, and you get jazz. Tune in to 99.6, and you get rock. And if you are just one decimal off, you get static. The difference is that your signal goes both ways. You are a sender and a receiver.

You put out a signal, a mindset of confidence about your financial success, and people, circumstances, and opportunities show up to support your success. When you put out a signal of doubt and uncertainty, you receive support for your doubt and uncertainty. You've been around someone you didn't trust or felt less than positive just being in their presence, right? You have also been around people that inspire you. That's what I'm talking about. You are projecting a frequency, looking to resonate with the frequency you are transmitting.

Anyway, the amazing part about these cells of emotion is that they are intelligent. They are thinking cells. These cells are constantly eavesdropping on the conversation that you are having with yourself. That's right. They are listening to you! And others are listening to your cells as well. Others feel what you feel when they are around you.

Your unconscious mind and cells are listening in, waiting to adjust your behavior based on what they hear from you, their master. So just imagine what would happen if you started thinking like Superman or a millionaire.

Here are some of the thoughts you might have during the day:

"The challenges I face today are easily overcome, after all I am Superman."

"I am indestructible."

"I have incredible strength."

"Nothing can stop me...NOTHING."

"I have supernatural powers and can overcome anything."

"I can accomplish anything I want when I put my mind to it."

"I can break through any barrier."

"I can and I will do whatever it takes to accomplish my goal."

"I fear nothing."

The trillions of thinking cells in your body and brain listen, and they create exactly what you tell them to create. Their mission is to complete the picture of the you they see and hear when you talk to them. They must obey. It's their job!

Since you are Superman, you cannot fail. Why? Your thinking cells are now sending the proper signal because you told them to. They are making you stronger and more successful every day! You have the ability to fight off all negativity, doubt, fear, and worry—nothing can stop you!

Superman has total confidence. So, your cells of emotion relating to confidence will now create more neuropeptide chemicals to promote feelings of power and confidence that others will feel in your presence.

Superman is fearless. So, your cells of emotion relating to fear will now create more neuropeptide chemicals to create feelings of courage. You are unstoppable!

And here's the key. Others will respond to you in the same way that you are talking to yourself.

If you are confident, others will have confidence in you.

You have thousands of thoughts every day. Make sure your thoughts are leading you in the direction you want to go. Ensure you tell your cells a success story and not a 'woe is me' story.

Most have been conditioned to think that creating wealth is difficult or only for the lucky few. What do you believe? It doesn't cost anything to think like Superman, and it is much more inspiring!

Mediocrity cannot be an option if you decide to be wealthy and think like Superman.

Your decision and communication with your cells create a mindset; that influences how you show up.

None of that old type of thinking matters anymore. After all, you are Superman, and you can accomplish anything.

If you want wealth, you have to stretch yourself. You have to do the things that unsuccessful people are unwilling to do. You have to say "yes" to an opportunity, then figure out how to get the job done.

Maybe you are uncomfortable selling and asking for money. If that's the case, then learn sales and learn to ask for money every day until you feel comfortable asking for it. You will never have money if you don't learn to ask for it.

I've learned a lot in the past 40+ years as an entrepreneur. I've learned that in order to have more, you have to become more. I've also learned that if you are comfortable, you are not growing. I realized that I couldn't go from being a nervous rookie speaker with minimal self-confidence to hosting TV shows and speaking in front of 5,000 people overnight. I simply wasn't ready. I grew into that, one speaking engagement at a time. Every time I finished a speaking engagement, I would ask myself, "How did I do it, and how could I do it better?" I still do that today.

And I've learned from the hundreds of thousands of people I've trained, coached, and mentored that none of us can do something we don't believe is possible. It won't happen if you're not ready to step out of your comfort zone and stretch yourself.

This has led me to understand the most important principle of wealth-building, which has meant the difference between poverty and riches for people since humans first traded for pelts.

Are you ready?

Come in just a little closer. Listen up!

Every income level requires a different you, a different mindset! If you think that $10,000 a month is a lot of money, then $100,000 a month will be completely out of reach. If you believe that having $5,000 in the bank would make you rich, then $50,000 won't miraculously appear. You will never earn more money than you believe is "a lot" of money.

What you do as a business is only a small part of becoming rich. In fact, there are thousands, if not tens of thousands, of ways to make money—and lots of it. I've learned over the years that focusing on who you want to become instead of what you need to do will multiply your chances of getting rich a hundredfold.

Ask anyone who's found a way to make a large sum of money legally, and they will tell you that it's not hard once you crack the code. And cracking the code starts with you and your mindset. The "code" I refer to isn't a secret rite or ancient scroll. It's not even a secret. It's a certain way of thinking and believing in which you've trained your mind to see money-making ideas.

That's where you see a need in the marketplace and jump on the idea quickly. It might involve creating a new product, or it may just be teaching others a special technique you've learned. It may even require raising capital to start a company or to market a product or idea on social media.

Don't Hold Back. You Have to Take Action to Change.

Start right now to imagine yourself as already having wealth. How would your life be? How would your day unfold? Start to own your wealth mindset now! The subconscious mind is unable to differentiate between fact and mere visualization. So, by imagining that you already have it, you're encouraging your subconscious mind to seek the ways and means to transform your imaginary feelings into the real thing.

Find yourself some mentors. Nobody has all the answers. Surround yourself with people who will support, inspire, and provide solutions that keep you moving in the right direction. Having a qualified mentor is essential if you genuinely want to attain wealth, have a thriving business, or reach the top of your game in any endeavor.

Okay, let's come in for a landing…

Having a crystal-clear picture of what you want to accomplish is essential before you begin. If you want to attain wealth, you must learn to operate without fear and with a sharply defined mental image of the outcome you want to attain. This comes from thinking like a wealthy person (like Superman), making decisions like a wealthy person, and being fearless (like Superman) when stepping out of your comfort zone. Look at the result as something you're already prepared to do; you just haven't done it yet.

Think about this. You have been preventing your success; it's not something you have to struggle to make happen. The key is not letting fear, doubt, other people, or mind chatter push your success away. You'll find that the solutions taking you toward your goals will come to you in the most unexpected and sudden ways. You don't need the *perfect* plan first. You need a perfectly clear decision about your success, the right mindset, mentoring, and the ideal way to get you there will materialize.

The most significant transfer of wealth in the history of the human race is happening right now. Are you positioned to get your share?

Remember, in order to get a different result, you must do something different. In order to do something different, you must know something different to do. And in order to know something different, you have to first suspect that your present methods need improving.

THEN, YOU HAVE TO BE WILLING TO DO SOMETHING ABOUT IT.

***

To contact Jim:

For more information on Jim's work:

www.JimBritt.com

http://JimBrittCoaching.com

www.facebook.com/jimbrittonline

www.linkedin.com/in/jim-britt

For free audio series sessions 1&2 www.PowerOfLettingGo.com

Max Willett

Max Willett is the CEO and Founder of Maxed Out, a powerhouse sales organization headquartered in Tampa, Florida. In the last 5 years under Max's leadership, Maxed Out has scaled to over 330 agents and 52 leaders that produce over $175 million in annual revenue. The agency has helped over 70,000 families nationwide and is driven by providing value to those in need of tailored healthcare solutions. Recognized as the #1 sales force in America in the private health insurance space, Maxed Out champions a "Givers Gain" mindset, prioritizing servitude and community impact. Maxed Out is powered by a strong purpose to help others achieve exponential growth, create passive residual income and unlock their full potential in business and life.

Max remains devoted to his mission of developing 200 leaders and scaling the company to over 1,000 agents who earn at least a six-figure income. Max continuously fuels his team with belief, energy and the power of a strong mindset. Living Maxed Out means putting forth your full effort to achieve the maximum results, which is becoming the best version of yourself and helping as many people as you can in the process. This Maxed Out Movement has created a unique culture of hungry, ethical, like-minded individuals that embody the entrepreneurial spirit and are obsessed with winning together to create the future of their dreams.

Living Maxed Out

By Max Willett

Success isn't about where you start; it's about the mindset and actions that drive you to where you want to go. My journey is proof that it's possible to overcome any obstacle and create a life of abundance if you're willing to put in the work, persevere, and embrace growth.

I grew up in Newport, Rhode Island, a small, tight-knit community surrounded by beauty and opportunity, yet tempered with growing up in a middle-class environment. My parents, Barbara and Tom, were loving, hardworking and instilled in me a deep sense of responsibility and ambition. They taught my younger brother Ben and I the values of discipline and perseverance, lessons I would carry with me through every phase of my life.

From a young age, I excelled in both academics and sports. I was a full-time scholar-athlete, balancing my studies with a competitive drive on the field and passion on the court. Competition fueled me. Whether it was academics or athletics, I thrived on pushing myself to win. But life isn't always smooth. It throws challenges your way to test your resolve.

My first major challenge came during my sophomore year of high school. I was playing strong safety on the football team, facing off against the number one team in the state. It was a game I had prepared for meticulously. But during one pivotal play, I tackled the opposing team's star running back. The impact was catastrophic. I remember the sound of my shoulder separating, the searing pain, and the realization that my season—and perhaps my athletic future—was over.

The diagnosis was grim: a third-degree shoulder separation requiring complete reconstruction. For someone whose identity was tied to sports, the injury felt like the end of the world. I was devastated. My self-worth plummeted, and I spiraled into depression. At just 15 years old, I began to turn to alcohol and unhealthy habits as a way to cope. I felt like the world had stripped me of my identity, and for the first time, I felt lost and didn't know where to turn.

But my parents, coaches, and teammates refused to let me stay down. They reminded me that my worth wasn't defined by one setback. With their support, I embarked on a grueling journey of physical therapy and self-discovery. Every session was painful, but each small step forward reminded me that I was capable of more than I thought. I returned to the field stronger than before, not just physically but mentally. That experience taught me a lesson I would carry with me for the rest of my life: adversity doesn't define you—it refines you.

After high school, I attended Rhode Island College as a student-athlete, balancing academics and sports. But after two years, I felt inspired to pursue something greater. I transferred to the University of Tampa, leaving behind the familiarity of home for the uncertainty of a new beginning. It was a leap of faith, one of many that would shape my life.

At the University of Tampa, I pursued a degree in exercise science and allied health with plans to become a physical therapist. To support myself, I worked full-time in hospitality, I started bartending at clubs and then moved to fine-dining restaurants. Bartending wasn't just a job—it became a masterclass in human connection. I learned how to communicate effectively, read people, and solve problems on the fly. These skills would later prove invaluable in building my business.

By my mid-20s, I was earning a comfortable nearly six-figure income in the hospitality industry. On the surface, everything seemed great. But behind the scenes, I was struggling. The fast-paced nightlife and all that came with it had taken its toll. I was drinking heavily, living recklessly, and slowly losing control of my life.

At 25, I realized that if I didn't make a change, I would end up living a life I didn't want and would lose the people I care about. I made the life-altering decision to quit drinking. Sobriety wasn't just about cutting out alcohol—it was about reclaiming my focus, clarity, and sense of purpose. It was the hardest and best decision I ever made in my life. I've been sober for over 10 years now, and it's given me the foundation to build everything I have today. I learned first-hand that adversity and hardship in life are truly opportunities for growth.

Then, in 2019, my life took an unexpected turn. While bartending at Eddie V's Prime Seafood, a group of sales leaders approached me with an opportunity to join their sales team. At first, I declined. At the time I had a very limited mindset and wasn't looking for change, challenge or new opportunities. I was comfortable where I was, and stepping into a completely different industry felt risky. But over time, I watched these individuals return for their winners' dinners to celebrate their success, which peaked my interest. Their energy, ambition, and sense of purpose were magnetic.

Eventually, curiosity got the better of me. I decided to take a chance. I joined their team, leaving behind the safety of bartending and diving headfirst into a new industry. Within a month, I was all in. I developed as a top sales agent and soon decided I wanted to help others have the same success. I stepped into leadership and began building my team, Maxed Out, brick by brick. Within five years, I had scaled my organization to over 330 sales agents and 52 leaders that produced over $175 million in annual revenue in 2024. Maxed Out is now the top-performing sales organization in America in the private healthcare industry. This transformation didn't happen by accident. It was the result of living by a set of principles I call "The 5 F's to Fulfillment."

The 5 F's to Fulfillment: Fitness, Faith, Family, Finances, and Fun

Success isn't about excelling in just one area—it's about thriving in every aspect of your life. The 5 F's are the pillars that have guided my journey and created the foundation of everything I've built.

1. Fitness: The Foundation of Discipline

Fitness is where it all begins. A strong body leads to a strong mind, and without physical health, it's hard to perform at your best in any area of life. But fitness isn't just about looking good or lifting the heaviest weights—it's about discipline, consistency, and resilience.

When you commit to a fitness routine, you're training your mind just as much as your body. Pushing through discomfort teaches you that growth happens outside your comfort zone. The discipline you build through fitness spills over into your personal and professional life, helping you stay focused and overcome challenges.

In my organization, fitness is a core value. We host fitness challenges, provide resources for meal planning and host in-office dinners with healthy cuisine prepared by our chef. We also offer in-office massage and chiropractic services as well as even connecting team members with fitness coaches. Why? Because I believe that generational habits are more valuable than generational wealth. By prioritizing health, you set yourself and your family up for success in every other area of life.

2. Faith: Connecting to a Higher Purpose

Faith is more than belief in a higher power; it's about conviction in your purpose and unwavering trust in the process. For me, faith encompasses my connection to God, but it also includes faith in my team, my mission, and most importantly, myself. Faith gives you the strength to persevere through tough times and keeps you grounded during moments of triumph.

During my toughest moments—whether it was overcoming my football injury, quitting alcohol, or starting from scratch in an unfamiliar industry—faith was my anchor. I didn't always know how things would work out, but I believed they would. That belief fueled me to take action even when the path wasn't clear.

In our organization, we emphasize the importance of connecting with your purpose. Every Saturday, we host an "Elevate Your Faith" session, where team members come together to reflect, share, and recenter themselves. It's not about preaching or imposing beliefs; it's about creating a space where people can reconnect with what drives them.

Faith reminds you that setbacks aren't failures—they're lessons. When you trust the process, you realize that every challenge is preparing you for something greater. It's a mindset that keeps you moving forward, no matter how uncertain the road ahead may seem.

3. Family: Building a Legacy Together

Family is more than the people you're related to—it's the community you choose to surround yourself with and immerse yourself in. For me, family has always been my "why." Everything I do is rooted in the desire to create a better future for the people I care about most.

Growing up, my parents modeled what it meant to prioritize family. They worked tirelessly to provide for us, but they never let that sacrifice take away from their presence and love. That example shaped my approach to leadership and success.

In my organization, we don't just talk about family values—we live them. Spouses are invited to winners' dinners, children come to park days, and entire families join us for company trips. These moments aren't just perks; they're a way of showing our team that their loved ones are part of our journey, too.

When your family believes in your mission, you gain a source of strength and motivation that's unmatched. It's no longer just about you—it's about building a legacy that impacts generations. And family extends beyond blood. On Maxed Out, we're a family. We celebrate wins together, support each other through challenges, and work as one cohesive unit.

Integrating work and family isn't just good for morale—it's good for business. When your personal and professional lives are aligned, you operate with clarity, purpose, and unity.

4. Finances: Creating Freedom and Impact

Our ability to communicate at a high level and provide value to our clients by ethically helping them secure the best healthcare for their situation is what allows our agents to earn such a significant income in this industry. Residual income is one of the most powerful tools for building financial independence. When we create coverage solutions for the clients we serve, this directly helps us earn income every month residually, in our sleep, forever. This is the reason why the insurance industry has created the most millionaires in American history. What's even more important is teaching others how to capitalize on this opportunity as well.

Financial freedom is one of the greatest gifts you can achieve—not just for yourself but for those who look to you for guidance. Leadership is key here because financial success isn't a solo venture. It's about multiplying your impact through others, empowering them to reach their goals while achieving your own.

In my organization, we focus on developing leaders who can create their own wealth while helping others do the same. This isn't just about teaching people how to help clients—it's about teaching them how to lead, how to build teams, and how to scale their success. Leadership magnifies impact, turning individual wins into collective financial growth.

Leaders in our organization earn significant incomes because they've mastered the art of empowering others. They don't just help families—they build relationships, foster trust, and inspire their teams to perform at the highest levels.

When you lead others to financial success, you create a ripple effect that extends far beyond your own life.

5. Fun: Celebrating the Journey

If you're not enjoying the process, what's the point? Fun is the glue that holds everything together. It's what keeps you energized, motivated, and excited to tackle each day.

In our organization, fun is a cornerstone of our culture. Every week we host high energy sales meetings, run team competitions and do daily raffles to uplift morale and team culture. From monthly winners' dinners to quarterly yacht days and annual international team vacations, we make time to celebrate our successes. These aren't just parties—they're moments that remind us why we do what we do and how fortunate we are for who we get to do it with.

But fun isn't limited to events. It's embedded in the way we operate. Our Maxed Out events are electric, filled with energy and inspiration. Our team dynamic is vibrant and supportive, creating an environment where people genuinely enjoy engaging with each other and giving their best.

When you love what you do and the people you do it with, success becomes inevitable. Fun is what turns hard work into passion and transforms a career into a calling.

The Ripple Effect of Leadership: Building Leaders, Not Followers

One of the most rewarding aspects of leadership is witnessing its ripple effect—the exponential growth that occurs when you empower others to step into their potential. Leadership isn't just about achieving personal success; it's about inspiring and equipping others to achieve success of their own. This ripple effect extends beyond the workplace, impacting families, communities, and even future generations.

When I first started building Maxed Out, I quickly realized that I couldn't do it all on my own. If I wanted to grow, I needed to invest in people. What I didn't fully grasp at the time was just how transformative that investment would be—not just for my business, but for the lives of the individuals in my organization. Watching someone go from being unsure of their capabilities to running their own successful team is an unparalleled feeling.

Many of the people who joined my organization had little to no experience in sales or leadership. They came from diverse backgrounds, some struggling financially or personally, unsure of what the future held. But through mentorship, guidance, the tools we provide and the systems we've developed, I've seen these same individuals transform into confident, influential leaders. Today, many of them are earning multiple six- or seven-figure incomes and have become servant leaders in their own right. They're not just thriving professionally—they're creating opportunities for others to thrive as well.

This ripple effect creates a cycle of growth and empowerment. When someone steps into their role as a leader, they don't just elevate themselves—they elevate everyone around them. This is done by leading from the front and showing others how to be successful through action and setting the right example. A great leader inspires their team to think bigger, work harder, and believe in what's possible. That team, in turn, influences others, spreading the culture of growth and success to the world.

On Maxed Out, this ripple effect has reshaped countless lives. I've seen team members pay off debts, buy their first homes, retire their parents and provide for their families in ways they never thought possible. But the impact doesn't stop there. When a parent achieves financial freedom, their children grow up in a different environment—one filled with possibilities and hope. When a leader gives back to their community, they inspire others to do the same, creating a wave of positive change that extends far beyond any one individual.

Leadership also creates a powerful sense of accountability and shared responsibility. When you know that your success directly impacts the people you lead, it pushes you to operate at your highest level. It's no longer just about personal gain—it's about fulfilling your role as a mentor, a coach, and a guide. This ripple effect of leadership isn't just about business growth—it's about building a legacy of impact and empowerment that continues to grow long after you're gone.

On a practical level, this butterfly effect fuels exponential growth within the organization. When leaders develop other leaders, they create a self-sustaining cycle of mentorship and success. Instead of one person carrying the weight of the team, leadership becomes distributed. This not only allows the business to scale but also ensures that the culture of empowerment and excellence is preserved at every level.

For me, the most fulfilling part of leadership is seeing the personal transformations that come with it. It's not just about financial success—it's about watching someone discover their potential and step into a life they once thought was out of reach. These moments are a reminder of why I do what I do and why leadership is so much more than a title or a role. It's a responsibility and a privilege, to serve, to uplift, and to create opportunities for others.

The ripple effect of leadership is one of the most powerful forces in the world. When you invest in others, you're not just changing their lives—you're changing the lives of everyone they touch. It's a legacy that continues to grow, impacting not just individuals but entire communities and industries. And that, to me, is what true success looks like.

Audit Your Environment

If I could share one piece of advice with someone starting out, it would be this: **audit your environment.**

Your environment shapes your mindset, and your mindset shapes your success. Look around at the people in your life. Are they encouraging you to dream bigger, or are they keeping you in your comfort zone?

One of the most important decisions you'll ever make is choosing who you surround yourself with. If you want to level up, you need to align yourself with people who already have what you want. These are the individuals who will challenge you, inspire you, and hold you accountable to your goals.

When I was bartending, my environment was one of comfort and complacency. I was surrounded by people who were content with where they were, and for a time, I let that mindset rub off on me. It wasn't until I started associating with ambitious, hungry, like-minded individuals that I realized how much more I was capable of.

Success leaves clues. Seek out mentors who can guide you, peers who can challenge you, and communities that uplift you. And if your current environment isn't serving you, don't be afraid to change it.

Maxed Out Blueprint

On Maxed Out, our mission is to put forth full effort and energy to achieve our maximum potential, becoming the best versions of ourselves. By doing so, we aim to continuously help others and build lives of abundance and freedom. Our company is built on our guiding principle of H.O.P.E. - Helping Other People Every day.

The Maxed Out Blueprint is rooted in three core principles: earning more income, creating greater impact, and having more freedom. This isn't just about financial success; it's about using that success to provide for your family, support your friends and loved ones, and give back to your community in meaningful ways.

Through initiatives like charitable donations, philanthropy, and community outreach programs, Maxed Out strives to make a difference far beyond the walls of our organization. We participate in supporting different local charities every month and donate over $500,000 annually to those in need throughout our community. These efforts embody what it means to create impact; not just building wealth, but using that wealth to serve, inspire, and uplift others. The freedom we cultivate extends beyond time and travel. It's the freedom to give, to serve, and to leave a legacy that resonates in our communities and beyond. This is the heart of Maxed Out: empowering individuals to achieve their dreams while making the world a better place.

With the Maxed Out Blueprint to success that we've built, there have been multiple millionaires and multi-6 figure earners created within this opportunity. Our leaders such as Brian Fuller, Chad Douglas, Seth Groff, Billy Pickhardt and Austin Baker have all become millionaires in just a few short years. Second year agents like Chris Mueller, Lucas Rodrigues, Joey Citrola, Austin Nichols, Brianna Hernandez, Scotty Binsack and Karalynda DeJesus all earn well over half a million dollars annually, as well as so many others. They have all been able to build better lives for their families and help support our community with the affluence they have created.

Our agency has over 150 agents earning well over $150,000 in their first year of joining Maxed Out. Our leadership team provides all of the training, resources and mentorship to help our agents succeed. We're fulfilled by helping others live with purpose, become financially free, and achieve their goals.

I want to take this opportunity to express the gratitude I have for our leadership team who has helped build such an amazing opportunity to change so many lives together.

Remember, you become the average of those you spend the most time with. Proximity is Power. Choose yours wisely.

A Call to Action: Your New Beginning

If my story resonates with you, and you're ready to take the first step toward creating the life you've always wanted, I encourage you to let me help you.

The life by design that you want is within reach—all it takes is one decision to believe in yourself and take action. Scan the QR code below or visit www.maxwillett.com to book a one-on-one discovery call with me. Together, we'll explore how you can unlock your potential, achieve financial freedom, and live a life of purpose and abundance.

This is your moment. Let's make it happen. Let's **Live Maxed Out.**

***

To contact Max:

www.MaxWillett.com

Bonita Palmer

Bonita is a proven leader, speaker, business growth coach and connector with over twenty-five years in corporate operations management and business ownership. Her focus is delivering exceptional leadership, empowerment and management practices in business environments.

Seeing the impact the 2020 pandemic had on so many businesses, Bonita felt compelled to bring that same level of operational expertise to the regional business community. She started BGP Group ActionCOACH to help business owners tackle the challenges they face every day: maximizing profitability, improving cash flow, creating better systems for business efficiency and hiring, training and retaining rockstar teams.

Bonita helps business owners create a business that's scalable and sellable so they can exit when ready and enjoy the life they dreamed of when they first opened for business.

Bonita holds Business, Executive, Corporate and CEO Coach credentials with the ActionCOACH Global Firm. She's certified in Business Training, the Harvard School of Business Foundations of Management, and is a trained Lean Six Sigma Greenbelt.

Bonita is an Amazon best-selling author of People Fusion. She has shared her knowledge and insights with hundreds of team members, business owners and community leaders as a keynote speaker and seminar presenter. Requested topics include: "How to Grow a Profitable Business," "Hire, Train and Retain a 5 Star Team," "Five Ways to Massive Growth," "Marketing is Math," "Fearless Leadership," and "Power of One."

The Ripple Effect:

Transforming Relationships into Business Success

By Bonita Palmer

What is a ripple effect? At its core, it's the idea that every interaction, no matter how small, sets off a chain reaction of consequences—positive or negative. In life and business alike, this concept isn't just relevant; it's fundamental. Every decision, every word, every gesture sends waves that influence not just immediate outcomes but far-reaching dynamics across relationships, systems, and even industries.

Some ripples feel inconsequential at first. I remember as a child visiting my grandparents' house and fishing in their pond behind the barn. When my bobber hit the water, it sent out rings of ripples. Later, we'd hike the canyon trails, yelling into the void to hear the echoes ripple back at us. Even jumping into a pool created ripples, waves dancing outward from where I'd landed. At the time, I barely gave them a second thought—those ripples didn't seem to matter. They were fleeting, harmless, and ultimately forgotten.

But as life progressed, I realized that not all ripples fade without consequence. The ripples of human connection—relationships with friends, family, and partners—carry far more weight. These aren't just visual disturbances; they're life-shaping forces. The closer the relationship, the more powerful the ripple. Bonds between friends can be forged or fractured. Marriages, seemingly impenetrable, can be strengthened—or destroyed—by a single ripple of trust or betrayal. Sharing a living space, a conversation, or even a moment with another person can set off ripples that alter the trajectory of your life.

When it comes to business, the stakes are even higher. The ripple effect becomes an unavoidable reality, defining the trajectory of growth, culture, and sustainability. Understanding how your actions create these ripples—whether they spark progress or provoke setbacks—is not just a skill but a necessity. Every interaction within your business has the potential to amplify your success or accelerate your downfall. To thrive, you must master the art of deliberate and positive ripples, because these waves don't just influence your organization—they shape the experiences of everyone it touches.

The Foundations of Trust: Why Ripples Matter

In the early 2000s, I began my career in corporate contact centers within the insurance and banking industries—fields that demand confidentiality and deep relational trust. These industries often require individuals to share their most private information: their health challenges or financial conditions. Many won't discuss such sensitive topics even with their family or closest confidants, yet they trust a stranger on the other end of the phone.

Why? It's because some businesses master the art of creating trust through their ripple effect. Every action, from the tone of voice on a call to the clarity of communication in a marketing email, contributes to a perception of reliability and care.

Contrast this with businesses that falter, where ripples of misaligned expectations, poor customer experiences, or disengaged employees can rapidly erode trust and credibility. In today's hyperconnected world, where instant reviews, viral social media posts, and public accountability reign supreme, these negative ripples can spiral out of control, shaping public opinion and consumer behavior with lightning speed. A recent, tragic example at the time of this writing highlights this phenomenon: United Health Care CEO Brian Thompson was gunned down in New York City. While the motive for this terrible act remains unknown, the ripple effect was immediate. Social media platforms erupted with speculation, opinions, and narratives. The tragedy became not just a personal loss but a reflection point for the corporation, with the actions and reputation of the business setting the tone for how the public interprets the event. This starkly underscores how corporate behavior creates ripples that resonate far beyond the boardroom—shaping perceptions, trust, and, ultimately, the future of the organization.

How Ripples Define Success or Failure

The ripple effect is not a new phenomenon, but its stakes have dramatically increased in the digital age. A single interaction, whether positive or negative, can echo across platforms, reaching audiences far beyond the immediate circle of influence. A five-star review might attract a stream of loyal customers; a viral complaint could result in financial and reputational damage.

Let me share two examples of businesses impacted by the ripple effect:

The Negative Ripple – A Case Study

I once worked with a young construction company owner who excelled in his craft but struggled with business operations due to lack of experience, business acumen and an Attention Deficit Hyperactive Disorder diagnosis. Financial pressures led to late payments, which damaged relationships with suppliers. Miscommunication with employees caused distrust, and inconsistent pay cycles resulted in high turnover. The negative ripples compounded:

- Frustrated suppliers refused to extend credit.
- Employees left, citing dissatisfaction and instability.
- Client deadlines slipped, leading to reputational harm.

Despite the owner's dedication and technical skill, the business closed within two years. This case underscores the cumulative power of negative ripples—they rarely stay contained and often grow exponentially, dragging even the most talented individuals down.

The Positive Ripple – A Case Study

On the other hand, I worked with an attorney dissatisfied with her role under a managing partner who undervalued her contributions. Determined to rewrite her story, she focused on creating positive ripples. She strategically networked, fostered referral partnerships, and consistently delivered value to her own clients outside of the partnership.

Within six months, the attorney's practice grew substantially. She transitioned from an undervalued employee to a thriving business owner. Over three years, she achieved a 285% increase in taxable income. Her success was not accidental—it was a deliberate cultivation of trust and strategic relationships.

These examples reveal an important truth: your ripples, whether positive or negative, amplify over time. The choice is yours.

The Mechanics of the Ripple Effect

The Starting Point: Small Actions Create Big Waves

Every ripple begins with a single action. For businesses, these actions range from internal decisions, like hiring practices, to external engagements, such as customer interactions. The key is consistency and alignment—ensuring every small action reflects your values and vision.

- *Internal Ripples*: These start with your team. A positive workplace culture creates engaged employees who, in turn, deliver exceptional customer experiences. Conversely, a toxic environment breeds dissatisfaction, leading to poor service and high turnover.

- *External Ripples*: These are the interactions with customers, suppliers, and the community. A single positive experience can lead to repeat business and referrals, while a negative encounter might discourage future engagement.

Momentum Matters: The Compounding Effect

Ripples never exist in isolation—they gather momentum and grow. A delighted customer doesn't just walk away happy; they become an advocate or a raving fan. They might tell three friends, post a glowing review, or share their experience on social media, sending waves of goodwill that can draw in new business like a magnet. But the inverse is equally powerful. A dissatisfied customer can unleash a tidal wave of negativity—a complaint that tarnishes your reputation, chases away potential clients, and even demoralizes your team.

Nowhere is this compounding ripple effect more evident than in sales. Consider this: it's often said that it takes 7–10 touches to convert a prospect into a customer. Yet, studies reveal that most salespeople stop after just five attempts, leaving potential deals on the table. But it's not just about persistence. The quality of those interactions matters even more than the quantity. Each touchpoint is an opportunity to educate, inspire trust, and build a positive relationship ripple that sets the stage for a win-win outcome.

Mastering Ripples in Small Businesses

1. Networking and Relationships

For small business startups, success often hinges on relationships. Whether you're working with early customers, suppliers, or strategic partners, trust is your most valuable currency. But trust isn't built overnight—it's the result of consistent positive ripples. Action steps include:

- Attend industry events and engage in authentic networking.
- Prioritize follow-through on commitments to build credibility.
- Keep the lines of communication open, follow up.
- Seek opportunities to add value to your network.

2. Team Building and Culture

As your business grows, the ripple effect extends to your team. The relationships you foster internally have a direct impact on customer outcomes. A motivated, aligned team will create positive ripples that enhance customer satisfaction. Engage these tips for success:

- Hire for cultural fit, not just skills.
- Foster open communication and celebrate team wins.
- Address conflicts promptly to prevent negativity from spreading.

Scaling Ripples in Larger Organizations

For larger organizations, the ripple effect becomes increasingly complex. Layers of management, diverse teams, and high customer volumes create challenges in maintaining alignment and consistency. Here's how to master the ripple effect at scale:

1. Hiring Practices

Your hiring process sets the stage for future ripples. A poorly hired employee can disrupt team dynamics, while a well-matched hire strengthens the chain. Follow these key practices:

- Craft job postings that reflect your culture and mission.
- Use structured interviews to assess both technical skills and cultural fit.
- Involve multiple stakeholders in hiring decisions for balanced perspectives.

2. Onboarding and Training

Many organizations underestimate the importance of onboarding. Orientation is about logistics, but onboarding is about culture. Effective onboarding builds trust, engagement, and alignment. Here are a few best practices to engage:

- Pair new hires with mentors to accelerate their integration.
- Use onboarding to communicate your vision and values.
- Provide training that empowers employees to contribute confidently.

3. Leadership Development

Great ripples require great leaders. Developing leadership skills within your team ensures that the ripple effect is intentional and sustained. Use these tips for leadership success:

- Invest in leadership training focused on emotional intelligence and communication.
- Create succession plans to prepare future leaders.
- Encourage leaders to model behaviors that align with company values.

Leveraging Technology to Amplify Ripples

Technology offers powerful tools to enhance the ripple effect. From customer relationship management (CRM) systems to social media analytics, technology enables businesses to understand and optimize their impact. Invest in technology and improve efficiency and effectiveness:

1. *CRM Systems*: Track and nurture customer relationships to ensure every interaction builds trust and satisfaction.

2. *Social Media*: Use platforms like LinkedIn and Instagram to share positive stories and reinforce your brand identity.

3. *Feedback Tools*: Leverage surveys and reviews to gather insights and address issues before they escalate.

The Ripple Effect in Leadership

Leaders play a pivotal role in shaping ripples. Their decisions and behaviors influence not just their direct reports but the entire organization. Great leaders understand the importance of leading with intention, empathy, and accountability. Identify in your team the traits of ripple making leaders:

- *Visionary Thinking*: They set a clear direction and inspire others to align with it.

- *Empathy:* They listen, understand, and respond to the needs of their team.

- *Accountability*: They take ownership of their actions and their impact.

Creating Lasting Ripples

To sustain the ripple effect over time, businesses must focus on long-term strategies. This involves nurturing relationships, adapting to change, and staying true to their core values.

1. Foster Loyalty

Customer and employee loyalty are the most enduring ripples a business can create. Invest in building relationships that last.

2. Embrace Change

Markets evolve, and so do ripples. Stay adaptable to ensure your actions remain relevant and impactful.

3. Measure and Reflect

Regularly assess the effectiveness of your ripple effect. Use data and feedback to refine your approach and amplify positive outcomes.

The Legacy of Your Ripples

The ripples you create today will define your legacy tomorrow. By fostering trust, nurturing relationships, and acting with purpose, you can transform small actions into waves of success.

Ask yourself:

- What kind of ripples am I setting into motion?
- How can I align my actions with my long-term vision?
- Am I building a legacy that reflects trust, growth, and impact?

Mastering the ripple effect is not just about achieving business success—it's about leaving a positive, enduring mark on the people and communities you serve.

***

To contact Bonita:

https://www.linkedin.com/in/bonitapalmer/

https://www.bonitapalmer.com

Carlos Hoyos

Carlos Hoyos is a senior global Executive Coach, Business Advisor, speaker, master trainer, author, and member of the Forbes Coaches Council. He specializes in leadership, governance, business strategy, AI, high performance, communication, accelerated learning, emotional intelligence, and networking. With over 25 years of international leadership experience, Carlos has collaborated with prestigious organizations such as IBM, Motorola, BNI, and BTS.

His journey is marked by resilience and determination. At the age of 14, Carlos was diagnosed with cancer, a challenge he courageously overcame. At 28, he made the life-changing decision to amputate his right leg to improve his quality of life and maintain independence.

He is a co-author of several business books, including *Team & Leader Coaching, ESG – Pillars For a Better Society, Brilliant Minds On Business Management,* and *The Advisors, Volume 3.* Since 2016, Carlos has hosted podcasts and online conferences, interviewing over 160 prominent leaders, executives, entrepreneurs, best-selling authors, and influencers.

Carlos's client base includes executives, C-level leaders, managers, entrepreneurs, and business owners. He has trained leaders from renowned companies such as IBM, Motorola, DHL, Hyundai, Mercedes-Benz, GE, Mondelez, and Aramco, among many others. His international influence extends to countries including the United States, Canada, Mexico, Brazil, the UK, France, Portugal, Spain, and Saudi Arabia.

Carlos Hoyos continues to shape and develop leaders worldwide, bringing his deep expertise to every engagement.

From Battling Cancer to Global Executive Coach & Business Advisor: Shaping the Transformational Leadership of the Future

By Carlos Hoyos

In leadership, the path we walk uncovers truths that the destination alone can never reveal.

My own journey — from battling cancer as a teenager to becoming a global executive coach and business advisor — has forged the pillars of transformational leadership that I share below. These pillars guide organizations through turbulent times and inspire others to achieve greatness. Becoming such a leader demands continuous growth, learning, and self-reflection.

As you explore the stories and lessons that follow, reflect on your own leadership journey and ask yourself:

What battles have you fought?

What pillars have you relied on?

And most importantly, how will you continue to evolve as a leader who shapes the future?

The Genesis of Resilience

In leadership and business, defining moments are not measured by titles, but by battles fought.

My first battle wasn't in a corporate boardroom but in the sterile corridors of a hospital, where I faced a challenge that forged the resilience, determination, and intentionality at the core of my life and leadership philosophy.

"We need to be strong," my father said, his face as pale as a sheet after a doctor's appointment that forever altered our lives. The X-ray didn't lie.

In the late 1980s, amidst global events like the fall of the Berlin Wall, my universe narrowed to the sterile hum of hospital corridors, the quiet wisdom of doctors, and the fight for each new day. Diagnosed at 14 with aggressive bone cancer, my reality became a relentless battle for life.

In these moments of vulnerability, I discovered the essence of resilience—not just of the body but of the spirit. It was in this hospital setting that I learned **the first pillar of leadership**: to be **Intentional**. I knew that surviving wasn't just about the treatment; it was about envisioning a healthy life. There is no real fortitude if you don't have a goal or a purpose.

I learned the power of determination, how purpose keeps you standing when everything else falls apart. Chemotherapy, surgeries, and recovery days taught me about resilience in its truest form. And then the **second pillar** — being **Informational** — proved vital. Every decision mattered, and seeking the best information available became crucial for survival.

This understanding of endurance backed by intention and information runs through every leader's journey, including those I've guided in various businesses.

Law Firm – Resolving Conflict to Rebuild Strength

At a well-established law firm, three partners—two of whom were a married couple—found themselves caught in personal conflicts and diverging business interests. What had once been a harmonious collaboration was now a source of tension, threatening the firm's foundation.

*They sought my guidance, not just for advice but for a path forward. Together, we restructured the firm, allowing the non-family partner to exit amicably and promoting a senior attorney to partner. This strategic move introduced new leadership and renewed alignment within the firm, reflecting the **third pillar** of leadership: **Strategic Intelligence**. With a well-thought-out plan, we navigated the complexities of personal and professional relationships, ensuring the best outcome for all involved.*

The transformation was profound. The remaining partners enhanced both employee satisfaction and overall productivity. The firm emerged stronger than ever, a testament to the power of resilience.

Just as I rebuilt my life after cancer, they rebuilt their business, proving that true strength often comes from overcoming our deepest challenges.

Rising Above: The Turning Point and No Return

By 2002, faced with a choice between a lifetime of limitations or amputating my leg, I chose the latter. It wasn't just about losing a part of my body; it was about reclaiming my life from the pain that had held me back. The decision was one of the hardest I've made, but it opened doors to new possibilities.

This concept of letting go to move forward was one I encountered repeatedly in my professional journey. The **fourth pillar**, to be **Intuitive**, played a significant role here. I knew in my heart this was the right choice, even when others doubted it. I can vividly remember when the nurse that was preparing me for the amputation said she would never do that kind of surgery.

The next story is about an ambitious architect who, like me, had to make a difficult decision to move forward.

Architect – Repositioning for Growth

An ambitious architect found herself constrained by limited revenue and partnerships that no longer served her business's growth. Despite her talent and creativity, she was stuck, unable to break free from the structures she had built around herself.

When she came to me, we redefined her business approach. Like my decision to amputate, she chose to cut off what held her back. We refined her negotiation tactics, and she recognized her outstanding service offerings, ensuring **Impeccability** *— the fifth pillar — in her execution.*

The results were immediate—her revenue increased by 30%, and she gained the clarity and confidence to propel her business forward. This case demonstrated that sometimes letting go of the old is the only way to make room for the new. In both our journeys, the courage to make tough decisions was key to unlocking a future filled with potential.

Crossing Borders: A New Perspective

The late 1990s and early 2000s were not only a time of global change but also a pivotal period in my career. In 1998, I left Brazil to work with IBM in the United States. This move was more than just a career shift; it was an immersion into global business and cultural diversity.

Although I had gained knowledge of diverse cultures as the son of foreign teachers, it was as an immigrant that I truly grasped the globalization of business and the need for adaptability. At IBM, my talents were quickly recognized, leading to opportunities that expanded my vision and deepened my understanding of global leadership, culminating in my nomination to the Leadership Excellence Program, an exclusive six-month course for the top 1% of rising leaders.

The lessons I learned about leadership on a larger scale were echoed in the experiences of a businesswoman running a quality consultancy.

Quality Consultancy – Empowering Leadership for Transformation

A businesswoman with deep expertise in quality consultancy struggled with low self-esteem and poor market positioning. Despite her skills, she couldn't translate her potential into success.

When she sought my help, we focused on empowering her leadership and repositioning her consultancy to highlight her strengths and value proposition. The transformation was remarkable—her annual revenue grew 3.9 times, and she fully realized her potential as a business owner. Just as my IBM experience expanded my leadership skills, her journey was about embracing her worth and stepping onto a larger stage. Leadership is ultimately about recognizing and harnessing the potential within, whether in yourself or your business.

*Here, we also embraced the **sixth pillar** of leadership: to be **Implacable**—getting rid of what was wrong in her approach while remaining compassionate toward herself and her associates.*

Return and Revelation: A New Mission

Returning to Brazil in 2006 wasn't just about coming home; it reignited my passion for developing people and organizations. With a global perspective, I was eager to apply my insights locally. At Motorola, I discovered my true calling wasn't in technology—it was in people.

Motorola, known for its innovation, was facing challenges in a rapidly changing market. Immersed in this new environment, I found myself at the forefront of a digital revolution where cell phones became integral to identity and productivity.

I also embarked on a personal journey, pursuing advanced studies in administration and self-development. This culminated in a transformative training experience in Chile, where I realized my potential and deepened my desire to grow and contribute.

The fulfillment of seeing others grow, reach their potential, and transform their environment was unmatched by any device or software. Then, the volatile technology sector presented an unexpected opportunity—a transition from a corporate career to entrepreneurship.

New Business Ventures – Reinventing a Struggling Business

A globally recognized entrepreneur in the franchise training industry found himself struggling with a new business venture. Despite his past successes, his new endeavor was facing low traction, and his team was not effective.

When he engaged with me, we worked on repositioning his role as an executive in this new venture, aligning his purpose with the business goals, and restructuring his team for better synergy. This process re-energized his approach and accelerated the company's formalization. Here, the **seventh pillar** *of leadership, to be* **Unshakable**, *was key. Developing emotional intelligence at a mastery level, turned the tide in his favor.*

The results were immediate—the program we developed together paid off from the very first meeting, proving that the right strategy and leadership can turn around even the most challenging situations.

Just as I reinvented my career upon returning to Brazil, he reinvented his approach to business, proving that with the right guidance, transformation is always within reach.

The Entrepreneurial Leap: Transforming Lives & Businesses

In 2013, after years of corporate success, I took a leap of faith and started my own company. It was a moment of clarity—an opportunity to merge my global experiences with my passion for developing leaders and transforming organizations. Though entrepreneurship came with challenges, it offered the freedom to innovate and make a lasting impact.

When I launched my business, my mission was clear: It wasn't just about building a company; it was a calling to create positive change, trigger transformations, and shape the future of leaders and organizations.

This entrepreneurial spirit is mirrored in the journey of a telecommunications executive who faced significant challenges within her family-owned company.

Telecommunications Executive – Building Influence and Authority

An executive in a family-owned telecommunications company was struggling to assert her influence. Her leadership and analytical skills were underdeveloped, limiting her ability to drive the business forward and gain the respect of her peers.

When we began working together, our focus was on strengthening her communication and persuasion skills, enhancing her analytical thinking, and making data-driven decisions. These developments were essential in helping her gain the authority she needed within the company. The **eighth pillar,** to be **Incorruptible**, guided us here—knowing her values and not turning away from them was critical in establishing her authority.

The outcome was extraordinary—a 48-fold return on investment. She not only professionalized the company's financial management but also solidified her presence on the executive board, proving herself as an irreplaceable leader within the organization.

Her journey echoes the entrepreneurial leap I took—both of us stepping into new roles with confidence, prepared to make a transformative impact on the businesses we were involved with.

Global Impact: Leadership on the World Stage

As I grew my company, my work began to take on a global dimension. Joining BNI, a global networking platform, was a pivotal moment. It wasn't just about building business connections; it was about leadership development and impact on a whole new level. I quickly rose within the organization, leading innovations and shaping the future of leadership training. Additionally, I organized an online networking conference with 42 speakers from 8 countries, further expanding my global reach.

In 2022, I took my global influence even further by joining BTS, a world-renowned strategy and leadership development company. Through BTS, I've been developing leaders and executives around the world, consolidating my international presence. This role has allowed me to work with top executives worldwide, helping them navigate complex challenges and achieve great transformations.

The importance of strong leadership and strategic alignment is a theme that resonates with a business owner in the beauty franchise industry.

Beauty Franchise – Revitalizing Team Engagement and Growth

A business owner in the beauty franchise industry was struggling with team engagement and limited revenue growth. Despite his efforts, the business was not reaching its potential, and the team's motivation was waning.

When he approached me, we focused on repositioning his leadership style, focusing on results, and restructuring his team to better align with the company's goals. This shift in strategy brought new energy to the business. The **ninth pillar***, to be* **Inspirational***, played a crucial role here. No matter the setbacks, we focused on getting back on track with a clear purpose, and reinvigorated both the team and the business.*

The results were outstanding—the business exceeded its revenue target by 40%, and the team's engagement improved dramatically. This case illustrates the power of strong leadership and a clear business strategy in driving growth and success.

Much like my journey with BNI and BTS, his experience shows that when leadership is aligned with vision and strategy, the results can be transformative on a larger scale.

Transformational Leadership: The Essence of Guidance

Over the years, my philosophy on leadership has evolved, matured, and solidified in focusing on absolute integrity, human connection, goal-oriented planning and strategic execution.

True leadership, I believe, goes beyond just managing people—it's about inspiring them, guiding them through transitions, and creating a lasting legacy. This approach has been at the core of my work, whether advising companies on succession or helping executives navigate complex decisions.

The importance of balancing personal and professional life was a lesson learned by a commercial director in the manufacturing industry.

Manufacturing Industry – Balancing Personal and Professional Life

A commercial director in the manufacturing industry was struggling with his demanding role, which left little time for his family, and his company's growth had stagnated. He sought my help, and together we focused on empowering him as a leader, optimizing performance management, and repositioning the company's commercial strategy. We also worked on time management to ensure he could spend more time with his family. The **tenth pillar**, to be **Incremental**, was evident here—recognizing that meaningful change takes time, and by making small, consistent improvements, we achieved significant results.

The results were transformative—he freed up four hours each week for his family, while the company saw a tenfold return on investment through better pricing strategies and increased growth. This case shows that with the right guidance, it's possible to achieve both personal fulfillment and professional success.

His story reflects my own journey of balancing leadership demands with the need for personal growth and fulfillment—an important balance for any leader aiming to create a meaningful legacy.

Shaping the Future

As I reflect on my journey — from battling cancer to becoming a global executive coach and business advisor — I see a mosaic of experiences, each one a lesson in resilience, leadership, and transformation. These experiences have shaped me into the person and professional I am today, committed to guiding others through their own challenges and helping them achieve their full potential.

However, this journey isn't about me—it's about the leaders and companies I've had the privilege to work with.

Accounting Firm – Resolving Conflicts and Fostering Harmony

Two siblings, co-owners of an accounting firm, were embroiled in conflicts that threatened both their business and their personal relationship. Financial challenges added to the tension, making it difficult for them to see a way forward.

When they came to me, we worked on aligning their purposes, mediating their differences, and developing their leadership skills. Through this process, they were able to resolve their conflicts and *focus on what mattered most. The firm eventually split amicably into two businesses, granting each side greater autonomy and the ability to pursue their own vision. Their personal relationship also improved, with a positive impact on their family life.*

Their journey, like mine, is a testament to the power of transformation—whether in business, leadership, or personal growth.

The 10 Pillars of Leadership: Checklist Review

These pillars are the cornerstones of transformational leadership, guiding you to lead with clarity, compassion, and unyielding purpose:

1. **Be Intentional:** Start with a clear vision. Know where you're headed and why, so every step is purposeful.

2. **Be Informational:** Seek out the best information available. Make informed decisions as the foundation of successful leadership.

3. **Be Intelligent:** Plan strategically. Align your vision with actionable steps to guide your journey.

4. **Be Intuitive:** Trust your instincts. Align with your heart and inner wisdom to reveal the right path forward.

5. **Be Impeccable:** Strive for excellence in execution. Ensure that your actions meet the highest standards.

6. **Be Implacable:** Address what's wrong without hesitation but maintain compassion for those involved to foster growth and integrity.

7. **Be Unshakable:** Develop emotional intelligence to a mastery level. Cultivate resilience and antifragility to withstand and grow from challenges.

8. **Be Incorruptible:** Stay true to your values. Let integrity be the bedrock of trust and leadership that inspires others.

9. **Be Inspirational:** Return to your purpose, no matter the setbacks. Inspire others to stay motivated and driven.

10. **Be Incremental:** Embrace small, consistent improvements. Understand that meaningful change takes time and is key to achieving long-term success.

Now It Is Up to You

In a world of constant change and rising challenges, leadership is the catalyst for shaping what comes next. As you tackle today's complexities, consider the impact your leadership needs to make.

And remember, you don't have to navigate this journey alone — together, we can refine your vision, energize your team, and drive meaningful change.

Shall we take the next step together?

***

To contact Carlos:

carlos@carloshoyos.com

https://CarlosHoyos.com

https://EliteLeaderInstitute.com

https://www.linkedin.com/in/carloshoyoslde

Ann Holland, PhD

Inspiring others to reach their full potential in their personal and professional lives has always been Dr. Ann Holland's mission. Ann's early years growing up in federally funded housing outside of Philadelphia inspired her and provided the drive to realize her full potential. Since then, she has dedicated her career to helping others. Ann earned her doctorate in Human and Organizational Development from Fielding Graduate University. In her 30-year career, she has led, mentored, and coached students, employees, managers, and executive leaders.

Holland is a dynamic and empathetic servant leader who has held executive positions in several industries and organizations, including Deputy City Manager for the City of Las Vegas.

Based in Greenville, SC, Ann is an ICF-certified executive coach, a member of the Forbes Coaches Council and a contributor to Forbes.com, a contributor to the Association of Talent Development, a certified facilitator, a professor, a guest lecturer, and inspirational speaker, the author of the book, Self-Motivation Mastery, and the owner of Strive Performance Coaching and Consulting.

Strive Performance Coaching and Consulting provides training, coaching, and consulting services, working with organizations, teams, and individuals to reach performance objectives. Using the approach of Conscious Development, Ann works with emerging and seasoned professionals to develop talent, building competence and confidence.

Where the Rubber Meets the Road!

By Dr. Ann Holland

Richard sat in his office, staring at the ceiling, his eyes bloodshot from countless sleepless nights. This was his first CEO position, and he had much to prove. He knew being assigned to a flailing tire manufacturing plant would be challenging. However, he also knew it could make or break his career. This plant had earned a troubled reputation for its dismal performance, and as a result, it was appropriately named by its previous CEOs as the "Dark Shadow." You see, every CEO assigned to the plant had left the company voluntarily or involuntarily.

The pressure to perform weighed heavily on Richard like a vice, squeezing tighter with every passing day. As the leader of a tire manufacturing plant, he was responsible for ensuring that production targets were met and every tire rolling off the line was flawless. But the harder he pushed his managers and team members, the worse things seemed.

Morale was at an all-time low, and turnover was high. People were leaving the organization faster than he could hire replacements. Mistakes were becoming commonplace, quality was slipping, and safety incidents were rising. Richard had tried every trick in the book to turn things around. He plastered the factory walls with motivational slogans, ran gimmicky contests, and offered incentives that fell flat. The cost per unit was the only thing increasing. Nothing inspired his weary team. Every night, Richard went to bed tossing and turning, consumed by thoughts of failure. He had to answer headquarters about why they weren't making their numbers, but even worse, he had to face the 2,000 team members who depended on him for their jobs. He never took it lightly that each team member had bills to pay, dreamed of taking a family vacation, and had kids they might like to one day send to college. He genuinely cared about the team members. However, he just couldn't motivate them to care about their jobs the way he cared about them.

One night, utterly exhausted, Richard finally drifted into a restless sleep. During the night, a strong and clear message seemed to echo in his mind: "Honor the wisdom of humility, authenticity, and honesty."

The following morning, Richard woke with a clarity he hadn't felt in years. He knew what he had to do. He called an all-hands-on-deck meeting, gathering every employee from the factory floor, the office staff, and his management team. He stood before them, not as their boss, but as a man laying his heart bare. At that moment, you could hear a pin drop. No one knew what he was about to say.

He spoke openly about his struggles, how deeply he cared for each of them, and how much he believed in their work. He reminded them that their job was more than just making tires—it was about creating a reliable tire so people could safely take their families to church on Sunday. It was about ensuring that countless people driving a car with the tires they produced would make it safely to their destinations. For the first time, Richard allowed himself to be vulnerable, humble, and honest. The sincerity with which he delivered his message was compelling and quickly captured the attention of everyone in the room.

Something shifted at that moment. The team members looked at him, not with skepticism, but with understanding. It was as if a light had switched on in their minds. They realized they weren't there just to serve the goals of a company or its leader; they were there to make a difference. Each tire they made carried their signature, a mark of dedication, integrity, and care.

Richard's words struck a deep chord with them. They felt seen, valued, and understood. Their purpose was clear, and they knew their work mattered to the company and the countless lives they touched by providing reliable tires. This renewed sense of purpose brought out the best in them. They worked with a new focus on their job and understanding that their work meant something. Whether they were a team member feeding the shift workers in the canteen or working the assembly line, for the first time, they saw their job differently. For the first time, they realized what they did every day mattered to Richard, the customer, each other, and their families. This realization that they were each a valued part of the process sparked a new sense of dedication, loyalty, and pride.

In the following months, the plant's transformation was nothing short of remarkable. It became one of the highest-producing plants in the company, with the safest record of any tire manufacturer in the nation. Richard had learned that true leadership wasn't about pushing harder; it was about lifting people, honoring their worth, and trusting in their ability to rise to the challenge when they believed in the work they were doing.

Where the rubber meets the road.

Richards lessons learned:

Holding a position of power and privilege can erode a leader's ability to relate to their team members. Leadership is most effective when grounded in humility, authenticity, and honesty. Leaders who prioritize these core values create an environment of trust and respect. When Richard had his "aha" moment and realized he wasn't connecting with the team members, he understood he needed to embrace vulnerability and foster a relationship of trust and understanding. Richard also realized he needed to help the team members understand their purpose and value. He knew that when team members have a clear sense of purpose, their work becomes more than just a means for a paycheck. When team members understand how their work matters, they feel a sense of ownership and pride.

Now, this seems like a wonderful success story, and it is. However, my responsibility as Richard's coach is to share a bit more about the story.

First, I must take you back to the day the team members began their cultural transformation. It was the day after his "all hands-on deck" meeting.

The air was crisp on this first day of fall, and Richard was feeling lighter and more excited than ever, but he was also anxious regarding his declaration to his team members. With his morning coffee in hand, he arrived in his office, greeted by a blinking red light that indicated he had a message.

"Hi Richard, it's Ann. I am thrilled to hear about your breakthrough. It sounds like you have had an 'aha' moment. I think now is a good time for you and me to get together and discuss a plan to move forward."

Sitting down at a local coffee shop, Richard and I, each with a steaming cup of pumpkin spice latte and a freshly sliced piece of pumpkin bread, settled into a discussion regarding where to go from here. "I am so glad that you called because now that I have made this declaration to all the team members, I must follow through, and I need your expertise to help me build a plan," Richard explains.

Sensing Richard's concern, I respond, "As we discussed previously, you have an opportunity to transform your culture." Richard nods and says, "Okay, that sounds good to me. How do we do that?" "Don't worry; I got your back. This is what I do." Richard takes a deep breath, sips his coffee, and relaxes back into his chair.

My question to Richard is, "I know how you feel about the direction you want to take the organization, but how does your management team feel about taking on this cultural transformation?" He takes a deep breath and cautiously assesses his management team's position on leading such a significant initiative. "I think they are still processing what this means to them, what will be expected from them as leaders, and how we will develop a strategic plan to lead the organization through such a transformation. They understand this is the right thing to do, however, they are concerned with the workload they already have, so, it seems a bit overwhelming to them."

Richard and I agree that for the management team to lead with humility, authenticity, and transparency, our approach will consist of thoughtful communication, building trust, and leading by example.

Richard grabs a slightly soiled napkin from under his coffee cup and starts to scribble a few ideas.

Richard immediately acknowledges that he needs to model the behaviors he wants his team to develop, starting with openly admitting mistakes and being transparent about his challenges. He also proposes that he proactively invites his team's feedback and suggestions. He commits to creating a safe space where his team can have "real" open conversations. Richard went as far as to establish "Transparency Norms" in meetings. This means no blaming or finger-pointing, learning from one another, honest reflection on challenges, recognizing others for their successes, and being vulnerable, humble, and transparent. Richard ponders for a moment and offers that linking values to strategy and success is critical since humility, authenticity, and transparency contribute to achieving goals. He continues, "Transparency builds strong relationships, while humility and authenticity inspire and foster loyalty."

Richard and I also agree that we need to provide the management team with coaching and training to help them develop soft skills like emotional intelligence, active listening, and constructive communication. As he is running out of space on the napkin, he jots down one more critical note: accountability. Holding the management team accountable for embodying humility, authenticity, and transparency would be crucial for leading and transforming the company.

Richard and I finish our coffee and leave our meeting excited and motivated. We understand that demonstrating humility, authenticity, and transparency at the management team level would mean creating a supportive environment where these values can be learned, practiced, and appreciated. Building this foundation with the management team will ensure these values cascade down through the organization. We have decided the next step is to involve the management team in developing the plan to move forward.

Key Takeaways

Humility

"Humility is not thinking less of yourself but thinking of yourself less." C.S. Lewis

Humility is a remarkable character strength. By leading with humility, leaders acknowledge their limitations and remain open to feedback, encouraging a culture where everyone feels valued and heard. Richard humbled himself to his team members by expressing empathy and compassion for their everyday challenges as workers, providers, and human beings.

Being humble means. . .

1. Empowering others: Giving up control and allowing others to make decisions and act.

2. Welcoming feedback: Not only does feedback provide leadership with different perspectives and diversity of thought, but it also boosts morale when team members feel their input matters and is valued by the company.

3. Giving others a voice: taking time to listen shows the leader values others' opinions and ideas and creates a safe space for open dialogue.

4. Celebrating the successes of others: Recognizing and acknowledging others for their contributions nurtures a positive and honest work environment.

5. Admitting when you are wrong: Holding yourself accountable shows a willingness to learn from mistakes.

Authenticity

"Authenticity is the daily practice of letting go of who we think we are supposed to be and embracing who we actually are." Bene Brown

Authenticity and honesty in leadership build a foundation of trust, credibility, and integrity. When leaders are genuine and truthful, they set a powerful example, inspiring their teams to act with integrity.

Being authentic and honest means...

1. Communicating openly: Communicating directly and clearly about goals, expectations, and challenges minimizes misunderstandings and helps create a culture of trust.

2. Making ethical decisions: making decisions based on values and principles that are core to the organization, developing a culture that is committed to doing the right thing, always.

3. Staying true to your values: No matter the situation, leaders who stand by their principles and don't change their behavior to suit the moment or gain favor gain credibility.

4. Being transparent: being straightforward in communication and action involves sharing relevant information. Being transparent strengthens relations with team members by providing clarity and openness.

5. Being open about intentions, decisions, and the reason behind the decisions: When team members are informed, they feel included, which encourages teamwork and collaboration.

Purpose

"When every action has a purpose, every action has a result." Greg Plitt

When team members have a clear sense of purpose, their loyalty and dedication to their work and the final product are significantly heightened. Take, for instance, the story of President John F. Kennedy in 1962 when he was visiting NASA. During his tour of the facility, he met a janitor sweeping a hallway. The President then casually asked the janitor what he did for NASA, and the janitor replied, "I'm helping to put a man on the moon." This powerful example illustrates how understanding one's role in an organization's larger mission can transform a job into a calling. When team members feel that their contributions are meaningful and aligned with a greater purpose, they are more likely to go above and beyond, stimulating a strong commitment to the organization's goals.

Leading with humility, authenticity, and honesty, along with promoting a sense of purpose, creates a positive work environment where loyalty, trust, and respect are mutual and collective success is the goal.

***

To connect with Dr. Ann Holland:

ann@striveperformancecoaching.com

https://striveperformancecoaching.com

https://www.linkedin.com/in/ann-holland-phd-9b57886/

Doug Giesler

Doug Giesler is an accomplished author, educator, and coach committed to helping individuals unlock their full potential and achieve extraordinary success while maintaining inner peace. Doug shares transformative strategies to UNLimit your Limit by overcoming limiting beliefs and cultivating self-awareness.

Drawing from his extensive experience generating top performance in business and uplifting others, Doug equips you with practical tools and techniques for personal and professional growth. His approach and philosophy centers on the concept of "Attuned Living" emphasizing the integration of mind, body, and spirit to create a harmonious and successful life.

Doug's warm smile, refreshing outlook and win-win philosophy are inspirational. Challenge your beliefs, embrace each moment as an opportunity for growth, and become the instrument of positive change. Join Doug on this transformative journey toward self-mastery and fulfillment.

Doug's proven methodology empowers you to break through obstacles and barriers, cultivate unwavering presence and awareness, master the art of conscious choice, and create your ideal future with unshakeable peace of mind. Each moment with him becomes an opportunity to evolve and excel, to elevate your life, career, and impact, transcend time-based constraints, embrace mistakes as catalysts for rapid evolution, and balance past wisdom, present action, and future vision, NOW! Crack The Rich Code. Unleash your limitless potential. UN-Limit your limit!

Unlimit your limit!

By Doug Giesler

Growing beyond previous peaks in life requires overcoming obstacles, fears, challenging limits while ceaselessly tested. Stepping into the unknown, a new "ME" must emerge! At times, we lack follow through, err, turn-away, avoid, and fail. With an energized, stable, unwavering mental framework, we can step forward confidently and enthusiastically by consciously embracing the unknown triumphantly!

The oncoming moment isn't known, yet due to comfort zones and personalized tendencies, we habitually bring our "known" selves into it. As we self-generate our inner constitution, we create laws and internal rules we follow unconsciously. False limited "truths", core beliefs, knowledge, and our <u>owned</u> definitions of our "selves" are problematic. By defining reality, we create labels that judge, measure, and set limits. Concealed behind layers of programming, they keep us the same vs. seeing and overcoming ourselves. Too often, we set it and forget it…NO MORE! That version of "self" is LIMITED! With awareness, and masterful presence, we can rise-up and UN-limit these limits!

By thinking, naturally we develop and imagine stories using words generated by beliefs we cherish.

Look within: words and stories LIMIT!

Mindsets stop at edges where we haven't done it or become it…YET! We must break through these thresholds, personalized walls, ceilings, and comfort zones. Words rule paradigms cemented in our minds with emotionalized, habitual imagery covertly packaged into moving "clips". We don't see them create limits; we see them as "our life" which is often self-generated unconsciously. We reconstruct the past and project variations of the future defining and "framing" this morphing reality. Our internals adapt instantly to the framework. Frames LIMIT! Thus, we arrive situationally pre-defined, and LIMITED based on how we are identified or "triggered" WITHIN! That's the unaware, unconscious mind. WAKE UP, it's a moving target.

Watchfulness sees this internal gearing attract, resist, avoid and RE-act accordingly. RE-act means habitually responding. We haven't upgraded our "selves", so we show up to life in similar ways. Once our patterns, magnetism and internal attractor factors are seen, they can't be unseen. Next steps are clearly revealed via awareness which highlights our "GO BIG" options. New actions are essential here as we evolve, otherwise, unconsciousness prevails, and growth fails.

Changing internals consciously changes our LIFE!

Seeing, hearing and feeling differently awakens new realities. Needs are revealed as awareness expands. Habits be dammed, we open-up, constantly learning to arrive every moment without our LIMITED "selves". Doing this effectively requires consciousness training.

PRESENCE PRACTICE.

"NOW" is the test. We must progress!

GOAL: Thief catching. Presence must catch the lower "selves" attempting the time thievery. Awareness of presence unlocks the NOW door empowering a stable and secure internal state: mind hack prevention mode. It's pass or fail! Represent as higher SELF vs. lower "selves" by eagerly observing this time slideshow.

Strategy window: NOW! Here's how:

Oversight. Watching the mind from above <u>AND</u> in it: Content.

Understanding. <u>Everything</u> happens FOR US vs. TO US: Context.

This receptive, highly aware state sees growth opportunities at critical life intersections. Presence with oversight via awareness offers CHOICE as we bring our new UN-limited SELF into each moment. That requires pinpoint timing, and unwavering self-awareness. Mastering this new perspective, <u>time</u> becomes an ongoing issue. Losing track of our "selves" within it, captivated for fractions of seconds and locked out of "NOW" is unacceptable. Virtual past and future "selves" steal presence in nanoseconds. BEWARE! (EGO maneuvering).

Claim, maintain dominion: Bring your highest, best SELF presently vs. allowing the lower limited self to steal YOUR MOMENT!

Letting go of past AND future "selves" enables choice, NOW…which affects ALL that follows. Wisdom creates idealized futures one choice at a time, but we get ahead of our "selves". We imagine, dream, want, see things "as if", producing and projecting impactful storylines within unaware and unconscious mindsets.

KEY REVELATION: A mind "set" is static, life moves. Don't "set" your mind from the past or futuristically. Set=limited. "Wanting" is a future "self": a LACK mentality. Double trouble.

Wanting, relative to TIME, means we don't HAVE the wanted. It's NOT true NOW, which feeds and DRIVES the future wanting "self". Beliefs matter; "want" mentalities believe in lack. STOP wanting, start having. Once dissected, awareness reveals that our "have not" habitual nature WANTS as a future projection vs believing in "have" NOW! If we had it, we wouldn't be wanting, "needing". See this behavior. Awaken to the beliefs that drive it: desires, fears within core mind "sets", unconscious beliefs tucked behind layers of emotional stories; pleasant, unpleasant, worthy & unworthy. Beliefs paint our world; we just don't see the paint or painter! Awareness reveals the painting process. Opportunities emerge to re-optimize, re-create, and masterfully become NEW by UN-limiting these "stories" CONSCIOUSLY!

Ego "selves" paint in STORIES.

RE-painting process: Address ONE LIMIT, one brush stroke at a "time", NOW! With attention, effort and focus, awareness oversees as we enter these life changing moments. Keying on time, awareness of presence allows detailed perception of when we toggle into the past or future mentally. Watching the intricacies and inner gearing of the mind from this more elevated perspective allows self-time-mastery. CHANGE happens as we constantly toggle back to NOW enabling CHOICE through personalized "AI" (Actualizing Improvement) Being above the mind and IN IT is like double vision operationally. While in it making things happen, we remain watchful from above, overseeing what the gears are producing. Separation and elevation with awareness allow us the mental structure to SEE, HEAR, and FEEL all at once: internally and externally. This "detached" perspective is less emotionally "attached" to stories which drastically expands our input and processing capacity: biased emotions aren't over-filtering, distracting or bogging us down. It's like seeing a whole paragraph from a more neutral state, instead of one word in a sentence. Context and content are simultaneously available, like a roadmap. The mind operates faster, more efficiently. We CHOOSE more effectively because more REAL-TIME, valid information is getting through via conscious presence. The wide-open eyes unveil an increasingly receptive and dynamic operating platform.

Once tuned, focus on the processor processing, observe where and when it skips, bogs down or repeats. This massively increases information flow and requires building up tolerances. Our ability to manage inputs and throttle data utilizing sensory capacitors is paramount. We get overloaded when we have not regulated and managed this influx effectively, our personalized circuit breakers get tripped. BALANCE is key. Freedom is attained as we observe, overcome and release the bottlenecks by increasing the amount of energy and data we can process without getting overloaded. Once our emotional circuit breakers get triggered, all bets are off because fight or flight mode shuts down the processor. We must learn where these thresholds are, and carefully perceive, sensing these self-created limits WITHIN! Diligently exploring, testing, working through these edges while observing our internal gearing and RE-actions creates opportunities where growth happens via IN-sight! Seeing and feeling imbalances, edges and thresholds, we observe the cause via context and the solution is instantly Self-evident! A limit generated by a lower "self" needs unlearning. As we rebalance, educate, and UN-limit that "self", we step into the next moment optimized and maximized, NEW! Miraculous transformations happen as we grow through each ensuing moment with amazing speed, mental agility, and stamina. We "become" less mechanical and learn faster.

Consistently achieving superior performance requires relentless, ongoing, energized FOCUS! Optimizing and prioritizing to maximize "becoming" is critical. Neutrality, balance and energized awareness at these junctures is essential if we are to UN-limit our limits. A fraction of these pivotal moments truly are most impactful. Fortunately, augmented awareness provides clues: <u>WHEN</u> to pay attention and fine-tune our immaculate perception capabilities. By emphasizing <u>THIS moment</u>, PRESENCE sees and recognizes self-imposed limits as they show up "wanting" to represent. Instead, our highest and best "SELF" arrives. Ultimately, we grow out of former "selves" that moment. Breakthrough psychology LETS GO of the lower limited "selves" that got us here right before the moment, on the crest of the transformational "time" wave.

This constantly puts us into situational opportunities for PRESENT evolutionary growth. NON-presence, even with effort, opens the door to mistakes and missed opportunities. The difference is that with awareness, NOW we see them. Here's where it gets interesting. Past "you" and future "you" are the ego generated "selves" that produce the limits that are seen ahead of "TIME"! We remember who we were and bring that "me" into the moment, or we project by imagining and defining a future "me" and BE THAT. This is now SEEN as problematic because BOTH ARE LIMITED, so we "SELF" correct the "self" that just arrived on the very edge of now, INSTANTLY! This happens right before we "click" into the next moment. Therefore, we don't "habitually" bring our limited selves into the moment anymore. We BE NEW instead! Being conscious, present, balanced and highly adaptable allows new choices based on exactly what is needed, NOW! We produce the highest and best ME, and that "I" considers an ever-expanding array of REAL-TIME information!

This progression enlightens and emboldens an overarching awareness within to highlight and observe past and future "selves" in commencing moments with ongoing watchfulness.

<u>BEWARE of detours</u>:

1. Present data is cut off.
2. Illusory information seen is lower "self" generated.
3. TRUE choice is unavailable; "mind-paint" blinds us via time blockages.

We can't make educated, fully informed decisions presently with REAL-TIME info if the mind is visualizing past or future data. Playfulness within watches this mind trickery. <u>Wanting</u> the known vs. the unknown using time as the accomplice, the mind thieves define the "known" pulling it from the past or projected futures. Observing this falsehood, we get back to NOW as the mind is "wanting" to decide based on past or imagined "knowns". Mind paint is rigid, illusory, LIMITED and we are often wrong by taking the detour. We miss it because we get caught up in emotions, ever-changing stories, words, definitions; attached and identified with labels in <u>TIME</u>! (Past / future.)

Labels LIMIT!

The way out: PRESENCE.

WATCH YOUR THOUGHTS!

<u>**SEE IT to BE IT**</u>: Wisdom grows through limited mindsets, observing every mind-tick, turn, success and failure with enhanced, dialed-up overarching awareness of mind operations and time intricately studying the unfoldment of life. SEE inefficiencies: where, when, how to do better, more, faster, harder, with more precision, focus, energy and PRESENCE! Mind tricks take us out of moments, cause mistakes, sub-optimal decisions and these failures are all revealed. With this constant influx of information, good and bad, we act on learned lessons, ever evolving rapidly. GET PRESENT and go after life as a BETTER SELF by consistently letting go of, and UN-limiting the lower self, FAST! Ten seconds ago, or ten years, we can't hang on to "failure" and show up NOW with an optimized and maximized higher "SELF".

LET IT GO and GROW!

To capitalize and learn in error scenarios, retrace your steps very quickly. In a highly alert and focused state, GRAB THE LESSON while still fresh and available! Understand the lower "me" that was "captivated" and stole the moment. The limited "self" was distracted…remembering or projecting. The presence was stolen, choice unavailable. It's FUN to observe and educate our "selves". It's progressive. We gain valuable IN-sights that amplify our self-awareness and productivity. The mind errs, we LEARN! Every intricate detail is noted in these time lock scenarios as that version of "self" tries to produce the correct "answer". The ego isn't NEW, it is "programmed", no two moments are alike, and programs don't work "universally". That is why we fail. The lower "self" doesn't belong here, now, we need to be NEW!

The "take-over" timeslot: Interjections happen between our highest potential SELF and the moment. By allowing this "detour" to happen right before now, we arrive defined and LIMITED. That projected or remembered self literally steals our life. Result: we stay the same. Presence outages lack mandatory real time data causing errors and delays. Once seen, noted and understood, we learn through the mechanics, internals, and "cause". No blame, no animosity: just peaceful GROWTH!

IN-sight: Instead of churning and burning emotionalized energy, (Venting, frustration, anger) we peacefully manage and direct highly charged energy to amplify learning through impactful growth opportunities.

Recommended demeanor: Focused, aware, calm, receptive. Graciously accepting, contextually balanced and contently energized. Mistakes are OK, studiously LEARN!

Emotional detours, resistance and avoidance miss learning opportunities via momentary unawareness. We PUSH life vs receiving it, see mistakes as failures, and get upset. Habits like blame, anger, frustration, and others prevent us from receiving lessons that would empower us to NOT make them again. Unconsciousness preserves the ego-self by bypassing moments. Thus, lessons go unseen, buried behind emotional storylines that blind us. Seeing habitual responses to life provides self-understanding. With IN-sight, we proceed in an increasingly UN-limited fashion vs. blowing through life unaware.

"THE WAY": Experiential growth expands consciousness evolving and enabling our BEST SELF! Achieve this masterful perspective, here's how:

1. **INTROSPECTION:** Define beliefs, ideals, dreams, popular stories and patterns. Identify, look behind, within cherished walls, ceilings. Dissect these mind curtains. What new thoughts could break you free?
2. **WATCH YOUR THOUGHTS PRESENTLY:** Highly awake and aware, FOCUS as you enter every moment. SEE the mind swerving, steering, resisting, avoiding. OBSERVE edges, look behind emotional cues, thresholds that arise in the mind. Tear down storylines causing mind wiggles and distractions WITHIN! When presence fails, retrace your steps, find out where, when, why, how and with whom the mind got captivated. What thoughts, emotions, triggers? Identify past & future selves, single out their THOUGHT-HABITS, catch them stealing moments!
3. **GET OUT OF THE PAST:** Observe where heavy emotions are in "time"? Re-gain presence: release the past after the lesson, take another step into NOW! Use presence, take deliberate ACTIONS!
4. **GET OUT OF THE FUTURE:** Mind generated future "attachments" grab our attention in nanoseconds. Notice the past mind "set" <u>becoming</u> a glorious or horrendous future mind "set". The future "ego" self is lightning fast, be FASTER! Attune to this past-future transitioning and notice the lower limited "selves" that slip in. What story, emotion, desire, fear captivated "me" and STOLE my moment? Learn the lesson, understand the drivers, transcend it, get back to NOW!
5. **ATTENTION TO DETAIL:** How long is presence lost in these "Time-traps"? Gauge the level of emotion, not to blame, but to SEE SOMETHING! (IN-sight!) Self-mastery of presence is the skill. This shows us the trigger WEIGHT, how important it is. AKA: NEED!
6. **NOTICE DEFENDING STORYLINES, habit-thoughts:** "Me" and "them" stories are created in a flash, driven by desire and fear which set LIMITS and attachments. Don't be deceived. With awareness, see attempted interjections on the

very edge of NOW. Be vigilant, hyper alert and conscious of these limited "selves" as they try to "hack" their way into the mindscape. Open-eyes, perky ears & senses…BE CONSCIOUS!

7. **REPRESENT: ACT vs RE-act:** SHOW UP as your highest, best SELF…NOT the habit-self. Re-actions are habitual, generated from "knowing": defined, former and future limited "selves". ACTIONS are NEW!
8. **FORGIVE:** Hugely important! When mistakes are made, forgive that lower self immediately! Get the lesson, LET IT GO, prepare for the next moment. Don't bog down in regret, remorse, anger, frustration, etc.
9. **EMBRACE THE UNKNOWN:** Be comfortable being uncomfortable. Excitement and anxiousness are emotional interpretations of desire and fear. Be willing, interpret growth as FUN!
10. **MASTER FAITH AS A TOOL:** Once understood, faith can be used to release future "attachments" allowing conscious steps forward with massive focus NOW. This eliminates resistance and "WANTING" while getting us amazing futures faster!
11. **TUNE IN:** Hyper-alert to "Mind-time-relativity" vs. NOW, focus on the heart. This connection provides notice of past and future "selves" alerting us as emotions get involved PRIOR to being "triggered"! That's why the heart must be dialed in and understood. It's "attached" to what we want, don't want, like and dislike. Enabling this incredibly powerful tool fine-tunes our gearing, interconnections and circuitry. The emotional clues provide valuable IN-sight, like seeing the future ahead of "time" as we arrive on the precipice of the NOW moment. That's precisely when we bump against internal drives, desires, fears, and meet our beliefs. Self-administered limits are revealed as ratcheted-up emotions enable awareness to HEED THE ALERT!
12. **ATTEND THESE INTERNAL BATTLES**: Pay attention, look behind emotional clues. When the heat is on, things are

ratcheting up, bring all your senses to the awareness party. The highest SELF must win this battle over lower "selves". Arrive in the moment, become NEW! The power of Now is maximized by using awareness and presence to step out of the self we once were. Fully aware, that limited lower self is UN-limited IN THE MOMENT!

13. **BECOME UNLIMITED!** Seeing growth happen in moments like this, WITHIN the awareness of pre-emptory emotions, everything becomes easier. Watching and observing reveals more lessons compounding growth and uncovering endless opportunities progressively. This shows us the gears that kick in prefaced by the thoughts, stories and beliefs that percolate up through the mind and body to be processed. These are DRIVEN by desire and fear, attractions and aversions. Highly aware and attuned to all that is activated WITHIN, we awaken to endless experiential opportunities for growth, always NOW!

Seek answers BEHIND emotions, disguised and driven by storylines. UN-programming requires mental muscles, oversight, adaptability, and SPEED with agility on the precipice of NOW to CHANGE OUR STORIES! Knowing where, when and how self-mastery happens allows being the instrument of change by capitalizing on opportunities within via higher IN-sight driven self-expansion. Arrive in the moment, affect change and BECOME NEW, NOW!

Develop these life changing methodologies and skills: enhance this growth-oriented mindset. Master your internals using key F-words to release the past and future alike:

Forgiveness + Faith = FREEDOM (Now!)

Break free from self-imposed LIMITS. Flex your mental muscles:

Forgiveness (SELF-LOVE): Let go of the past.

Faith (SELF-TRUST) Let go of the future.

BE FREE, with masterful awareness, IN-sight and presence, UN-limit your limits as they are seen, NOW is how! ☺

***

To contact Doug:

For a FREE GIFT, The Limit-Breaker's Blueprint. Visit: www.UNlimityourlimit.com/limitbreakers

UNLimityourlimit.com

WhatTheFWords.com

Doug@DougGiesler.com

Daniela Man

Daniela is an expert in complementary and alternative medicine, a nutritionist, a Rapid Transformational Therapist, a Transformational Coach, an author, and a speaker. She has helped thousands of people around the world break free from subconscious limiting beliefs and create the lives they have always wanted.

Her passion for empowering others began when she successfully helped her own child overcome a severe health condition and regain his ability to speak through specific dietary changes and various other modalities. Daniela shares these approaches on her personal website and across her media platforms.

She is the founder of The Cellular Memory Reset®, The Mind Of The Gut® and The Identity Codes™, which offer her unique methods for achieving fast, profound, and lasting transformations at the level of thoughts, emotions, and DNA expression.

Daniela's fascination with science has led her to collaborate with some of the world's leading scientists to conduct a proof-of-concept study on cellular memory. This research aims to explore how thought alone can activate healing genes in the human body.

Daniela is dedicated to helping people create new positive neural pathways in their brains and activate the right genes for healing, connection, abundance, and the freedom to be their true selves. Additionally, she assists others in achieving coherence within their body's electromagnetic field. After all, before we were cells, we were energy.

Cellular Reset: Unlocking Your Full Potential for Success

By Daniela Man

I struggled for weeks to narrow down this chapter, wrestling with the question: *What do I truly want to leave you with, dear reader?* I wanted to offer you more than just a deeper understanding of success. I wanted to give you tools—practical, transformative tools—that you can apply to your own life.

But as I sat with this intention, I found myself hesitating. I told my husband, *"I'm unsure what to say because I haven't yet arrived at where I want to be."*

He looked at me with kindness and said, *"My darling, it's not about where you are today; it's about where you started. Remember those days when you had to open the fridge in complete silence, and there was so little in it? Remember being told to slice the salami paper-thin so it would last longer?"*

His words struck a deep chord in me. I had completely forgotten. Forgotten the days of scarcity, when even daily food was a source of worry. Forgotten my fear of the fridge, a fear rooted in knowing how little it held.

There were days when we had to make a few small provisions stretch for as long as possible. Days when my father's depression hung over our small apartment like a heavy fog, and we moved quietly so as not to disturb his pain. Days when my mother sought comfort in the bottle, and I became her quiet protector, always watching, always on edge.

Those memories felt like a lifetime ago. And, in many ways, they were.

I grew up with my grandmother in a small cottage in a communist country, where self-expression and abundance were neither permissible nor imaginable. She had survived war and famine, scars that ran deep in her soul. She waited years for my grandfather to return from the war, and she was among the lucky ones—he did come home.

But when he finally arrived, she barely recognized him. The man she had known—the one who had left—never truly returned. He was a shadow of himself, and she was left to shoulder the burdens of the household alone: the children, the farm, the finances.

Despite the challenges, my grandmother surrounded me with love. We had little in terms of material wealth, but I never felt poor. Not for a single moment. The children in our village might have laughed and called us poor, but their words didn't touch me. I had love. I had freedom. And I had the space to simply *be myself.*

Years later, I packed my things and set out to explore the world, creating a life filled with joy and abundance—or so I believed. I truly thought I had it all.

I had love, a beautiful family, financial stability, and a promising corporate career. From the outside, it looked perfect. But inside, something was missing. There was an emptiness I couldn't explain, a yearning for a connection I couldn't define.

Everything changed when my second child was born. My world was turned upside down after he had a severe and life-altering reaction to a medical intervention. Sleepless nights stretched into weeks of suffering and desperation. We sought help from countless specialists, only to be told that he would never fully recover. They said I needed to accept it and move on.

In that moment, the "ideal" life I thought I had built came crashing down. I felt defeated, confused, and abandoned. Anger welled up inside me—anger at *life itself*!

There was no one who could guide me, no one who truly understood what I was going through. I was in a foreign country with two very young children, and my husband, overwhelmed by the weight of it all, began to withdraw. He found work away from home, leaving me to face the challenges alone.

I left my job to care for my son, who now required constant attention. With no steady income, our finances dwindled. I knew I had to find a way to build something from home, to support my children while still being present for them.

Our home was filled with tears, pain, and fear—fear that this would be our reality forever. Fear that I had been abandoned by the world, left to fend for myself. Fear that I simply wasn't enough to rise above it all.

Then came the day when I hit rock bottom.

I opened the fridge, and it was empty. The memories of another lifetime rushed in. My bank account was expecting funds that had not yet arrived. I went to my son's piggy bank and took the coins he had saved so I could buy food.

With those I bought potatoes and eggs. That night, we boiled them and ate them with salt. There wasn't even enough money for oil to fry them.

That day, I realized how far I had fallen. That day I decided that I was never going to be so broke and broken again.

It was almost like there was another me, deeply buried within and she became alive that day.

It felt as if I were standing outside myself, looking in at my life.

How did this happen? I asked myself. *How did I come to feel so helpless, so lost?*

I fell to my knees, surrendering completely, and asked for help with every cell in my body and every ounce of my being.

In that moment, I felt a strength I had never known before. A realization washed over me: the power I needed wasn't outside of me—it was within.

From that day on, I stopped looking outward for answers. I stopped searching for solutions in the world around me and turned my focus inward.

I had read countless self-development books. I completed course after course, devoting myself to daily meditation. I had learned from incredible teachers—some of the most successful people on this planet.

Success to me meant having it all—and having it all at the same time. To me, that meant not only financial stability and my son's healing but also having support, community, and the freedom to follow my heart's desires. It meant spending quality time with my children and the people I loved, healing my relationship with my husband, and enjoying life's simple pleasures.

It meant having healthy nourishing food available at any time, traveling to beautiful places, by the sea, in the sun, building a soul-led business.

In my journey, I had seen enough wealthy people to understand this: wealth alone does not equal abundance. Abundance, to me, is the freedom to *be*, *do*, and *have* whatever your heart truly desires.

I didn't just want to be wealthy. I wanted to be abundant.

And success, as I came to define it, meant precisely that—having it all, all at the same time.

But here's what I realized: all of that had to come from within. I couldn't just wish for abundance; I had to *become* abundant.

And to do that, I had to believe it was possible—for *me*.

That was the hardest part.

I grew up hearing that certain things simply weren't available to "people like us." I was taught that while others might live extraordinary lives, our family wasn't destined for such things.

I was conditioned to believe that success came through a predictable formula: go to school, study hard, work even harder, climb the corporate ladder, and eventually, you'd earn the reward—a comfortable life.

But life doesn't work that way.

The Universe doesn't give us what we want. It gives us what we *believe*. At the time, I didn't know that.

Worse still, I didn't believe I was worthy of having it all.

I didn't believe I was a good enough mother. I carried immense guilt for choosing the doctor whose decision led to my son's injury. The shame of that weighed heavily on me.

I didn't feel good enough—not as a mother, not as a person. I wasn't smart enough, wise enough, or capable enough to shield my family from the pain and suffering we were experiencing. And no matter how hard I worked, there were still days when the fridge was empty.

But on that pivotal day, when I faced the emptiness again, I understood something deeper.

Everything—*everything*—had to start with me.

It had to start with the message I was sending out to the Universe. Because the truth is, the Universe speaks only one language: frequency.

And here's the thing: the Universe never says *no*.

Whatever you believe—about the world, about others, and most importantly, about yourself—becomes your reality.

We are the co-creators of our lives, both the observer and the observed. The beliefs we carry within us shape the lives we live.

Quantum physics has always fascinated me. I spent countless hours reading, researching, and exploring its principles.

At that point, I made the decision that my life was about to start anew. I was going to create a life overflowing with abundance, joy, love, and freedom—the freedom to do whatever I wanted, wherever I wanted, and with whomever I chose.

I knew that it was up to me, and only me, to make this dream a reality.

When we change our beliefs, we change our lives. It's as simple—and as profound—as that. Our beliefs inform our reality. What we believe, we become. What we believe about life, we create more of.

Every day, I focused my attention on the truths I wanted to manifest. Without fail, I meditated deeply, visualizing my ideal life and circumstances. Importantly, I let go of attachment to specific outcomes. Instead, I surrendered to the idea that the Universe knew best and would show me the way.

I started playing a little game with my husband. He and I would stroll along the marina, pretending to shop for a boat. At the time, I didn't even own a car, let alone have the money for a boat. Yet we would walk hand in hand, role-playing as if we were deciding which boat was best for us. Afterward, we'd stop at the boat club for a cappuccino. Often, we could only afford one cappuccino each and a shared lava cake, but I loved the energy of that space.

I loved watching the people on their boats, imagining myself as one of them. In my mind, I *was* one of them. I daydreamed, fully immersing myself in the possibility.

I also envisioned my son perfectly healthy, his digestion flawless, smiling with pure joy. I visualized him speaking confidently, engaging with those around him, and thriving in ways that once felt out of reach.

At that time, my son's reality was very different. His inflammation was severe, his digestion fragile. He spoke only a few words and isolated himself from everyone except me and his older brother.

But then, things began to shift. My husband came back to us, becoming more present and supportive than ever.

Soon after, we received an invitation from our son's school to discuss his progress. To our astonishment, they reported a sudden and remarkable transformation. Our son was not only speaking, playing, and communicating, but excelling academically. He was so quick to answer test questions that the computer administering the test struggled to keep up. The teachers discovered he had perfect pitch and encouraged us to nurture his musical talents.

He was making friends, radiating love, and embracing life.

The school staff wanted to know what we had done. They knew we had pursued biomedical treatments in the past and were curious about the new treatment.

I shrugged, unsure of what to say. Then my husband turned to me:

"But you've been doing all those meditations."

His words stopped me in my tracks. Could it really be that my inner work—the meditations, the intention-setting, the current focus—were creating such profound, tangible results?

That realization motivated me like nothing else. I doubled down on my meditation practice and my research.

Not long after, I received an unexpected phone call. A collaboration opportunity came my way, offering an income in one month that matched what I used to earn in an entire year. All this during the start of 2020, when the world seemed to be shutting down and businesses were closing their doors.

My business flourished. The connections I was making brought healing and renewal—not just for my son, but for my entire family.

I found myself working less while earning more.

I had more time to spend with my husband, and our relationship began to heal.

And the boat I once pretended to shop for during our marina walks? It was now a reality I could pay for in cash.

I went back to my research, and what I discovered amazed me. Not only can we amplify our lives by believing in what we are creating, but there's a way to go even deeper—by learning to communicate with our own DNA and compel it and instruct it to help us change not just our bodies but the outcome of our own lives.

DNA is the body's expression of consciousness. We are all spiritual beings having a human experience in this 3D world. We only perceive a small part of reality because our DNA, with its two strands, is conditioned to do so.

When scientists mapped the human genome, they were unable to understand about 98% of our DNA. They called it "junk DNA" because they couldn't find any correlation between those parts of the genome and known diseases or functions.

But nature doesn't create anything for no reason—especially not something so vast. I believe that in time, we'll discover that the key to complete healing and creation lies within this so-called "junk DNA."

There have been countless instances of spontaneous healings, and when you look at the work of experts like Dr. Bruce Lipton, Dr. Joe Dispenza, Gregg Braden and Marisa Peer, to name a few, it becomes clear that there is a scientific explanation for these miracles. Our bodies respond to our thoughts. And our thoughts shape our biochemistry.

When we change our thoughts, we change the biological and chemical interactions in our bodies, which ultimately change the signals between our cells. Our genes don't activate on their own—they need a signal to do so, much like a remote control tells a TV what channel to display.

This signal determines which genes become active and which stay dormant. It tells genes to create proteins and influence other genes based on the information it receives from our environment and, most remarkably, from our thoughts.

The Immediate Early Genes (IEGs), take just three seconds to reach full expression, control the expression of hundreds of genes and thousands of proteins in our bodies and can be triggered by thought alone.

Yes, our thoughts alone can signal genes. And our thoughts also signal the field of potentiality, which is Life itself, bringing experiences to us, based on our own belief system.

In other words, our beliefs shape our reality.

Cellular programming was first proven by Dr. Bruce Lipton more than 30 years ago, and today it's being confirmed in new studies in quantum biology and quantum physics.

So, yes—our thoughts can make us sick, depressed, or poor. But they can also help us heal and create the life we've always dreamed of. Our free will exists in our own DNA.

We get to decide which thoughts we want to cultivate in our mind, just like a gardener decides which plants to bloom in their garden.

Recently, scientists from Harvard and Vienna made a groundbreaking discovery. They found that certain genes, when suppressed, can erase a cell's memory, making the cell more open to reprogramming. This not only makes the reprogramming process faster but also more effective. (You can read the full article here: https://www.nature.com/articles/nature15749)

And in 2023, Science Direct published a study that proved how mentally focusing on collapsing a wave into a particle directly influences physical systems. (Here's the study: https://www.sciencedirect.com/science/article/abs/pii/S0079612323000286)

What this means is fascinating: all particles exist in multiple states at once. They are both matter and energy at the same time. A particle exists everywhere, as an infinite possibility, until it's observed.

This process is called "collapsing the wave-function." When observed, the wave-function collapses into the most likely option—a particle, which is fixed in space and time. When it's no longer observed, the particle returns to the state of possibility, becoming nonlocal in both space and time.

This means the observer—the person watching—actually changes the outcome of whatever is being observed, based on their expectations.

Based on all this knowledge, I completely changed my life and the outcome of my son's journey. And I wanted to give back and share this with the world.

So, I developed a simple method that helped thousands of people around the world heal from chronic conditions, overcome traumatic events, and create the life they've always dreamed of.

This method is called The Cellular Memory Reset, and you can learn more about it at thecellularmemoryreset.com

Today, dear reader, I want to leave you with this: you are the creator of your own reality, and you can heal your life. No matter what you're dealing with right now, no matter what you're going through, no matter what your story is. Because you are not what happened to you, you are not your thoughts or your emotions.

You are the one who is watching.

Go within and remember that you are empowered. You are enough, exactly the way you are, and worthiness is your birth right.

We get what we expect, so expect abundance. Expect freedom. Expect healing. Expect miracles.

Act every day towards your own dreams as if they have already come true.

You can have it all and you can have it all, all at the same time.

Believe it and it becomes real to *you*.

***

To contact Daniela:

https://danielaman.life/

https://thecellularmemoryreset.com/

https://www.instagram.com/danielaman.life/

https://www.facebook.com/danielamantransformationalcoaching/

daniela@danielaman.life

acasaladaniela@gmail.com

https://acasaladaniela.ro/

Luannah Victoria Arana

Luannah Victoria Arana is a transformational coach, healer, and bestselling author with over 30 years of experience in trauma recovery and personal empowerment. Drawing from Hawaiian wisdom, sound healing, and movement therapy, she helps women heal deeply and reconnect with their authentic selves, guiding them toward lives of purpose and joy.

A world traveler and #1 Bestselling Author, Luannah is the founder of the SoulSpectives Institute for Personal Transformation and owner of Serenity By The Sea Retreats on the West Coast of British Columbia. Passionately dedicated to empowering women, she integrates her extensive training in diverse spiritual and healing traditions from around the globe. At her transformative retreat center, she creates nurturing spaces where women can unlock their potential, embrace their gifts, and cultivate self-mastery.

Luannah's work is deeply rooted in nature-based wisdom, and her unique approach inspires profound shifts in those she guides. She is excited to launch the SoulSpectives Institute Coaching app, offering valuable resources and a supportive community for those seeking empowerment and growth.

Through her retreats, coaching programs, and unwavering dedication, Luannah has empowered countless women to recognize their inner power and transform their dreams into reality.

The Power and Possibility of You!

By Luannah Victoria Arana

Do you ever feel like, no matter what you do, you just can't seem to break through to the next level that you sense is over the horizon, personally or professionally? Perhaps you feel frustrated for applying various strategies, teachings, and techniques, yet the needle doesn't move. Do you sometimes feel so stuck that you just want to drop everything and disappear?

You Are Not Alone

I can't count on both hands the number of times I've felt that way, where I literally dropped to my knees, questioning myself and my life, thinking there must be something wrong with me because things were not working as I thought they should. Ironically, after many times getting back on my feet, I discovered that what actually keeps us stuck—something we too frequently fail to recognize—is that these moments and feelings are a natural part of our evolutionary process. That very pressure at the precipice of frustration and desperation acts as a catalyst for new thought and creation. Instead of fighting these emotional triggers, we need to embrace them as feedback, indicating a redirect is needed. Perhaps new information needs to be acquired, or new creative actions need to be explored.

Understanding the Dynamics

We are constantly faced with new challenges that stir up our inner underworld, giving rise to a multitude of thoughts, emotions, perceptions, and feelings each day. They shake us and sometimes break us to the point where all we want to do is give up. The next step feels impossible because we can't yet clearly see it. This is where we need to remind ourselves of two important facts: You are not just a mind; you are also a soul, which has access to insights and innate wisdom that the mind cannot reach on its own. And that we live in a world of contrast and duality, which will never change. What's not natural is the belief that challenges, and "failure" should not happen, and that life should be smooth and challenge-free.

When we feel squeezed and triggered by circumstances and situations showing up in our lives, much more is happening beneath the surface, making it seem as if we have no control. In this unexpected storm of chaos and emotions, we tend to lose sight of our inner True North, the guide to our true authentic self, experienced in those precious moments where you land in a sweet spot within you where you feel, ya, this is me, I feel good. When we disconnect from that feeling, driven by false beliefs and fears, it can feel like we become someone we do not know. Then, once the storm passes, we often brush it off as just a mood, never really addressing the root of what transpired. We can feel powerless, believing that the possibilities of a better future are out of reach. Yet, this feeling couldn't be further from the truth in those breakdown moments. The trick is to develop the inner mindset muscle to remember this, in moments when we feel squeezed and triggered. Building the Mindset Muscle to direct our thoughts intentionally in those instances, rather than being governed by unconscious beliefs that often set us up as victims at the mercy of our circumstances.

The Importance of Addressing These Challenges

Embracing life with this understanding—especially in moments of challenge and even extreme traumatic experiences of loss and abuse that I have lived and grown through—has brought me through my dark nights of the soul, step by step, continually showing up to grow beyond where I was to ultimately be living the life of my heart's deepest longing, against all odds. By societal standards, I shouldn't be as successful as I am. I didn't follow prescribed pathways to success; I always followed the call of my soul, down many rabbit holes, through many twists and turns, which, through each challenge, brought me face-to-face with the unconscious beliefs and patterns limiting my perception of myself, others, and life in general that kept me looping in the same stories and scenarios for too long. It took a lot of inner work, though, to listen to my soul. I struggled within myself with the contrast in me where, on one side, I have always felt and known a connection to God/Goodness and universal spiritual principles, but my biology was riddled with buried trauma patterns, locked in survival mode. These traumas created a hypersensitive nervous system in me, catalyzing emotions of fear that would often hijack my 'higher knowing'. I would short circuit in one of two ways: plummeting into the dungeon of D's, Doubt, Despair, and Depression, or the Triple-A reactions of Anxiety, Anger, and Aggression. This was so confusing until I started learning about trauma biology. I discovered that the only way to stay aligned with my heart and soul was to understand my biology to heal my body and bridge the gap between my true nature and the survival nature that took over. I discovered that my spirituality was not enough to heal me.

I needed to heal my body and come out of survival mode in order to fully embody my soul to stay connected to the warmth and comfort of God within my heart. I have always strongly believed in the good in life and in love. Not Fairytale Faith, which is beautiful, too. Faith-based in facts. The facts of immutable universal laws that govern all creation including us. 'There but for the Grace of God go I.' God is the force of goodness and love that is the foundation of all that is and all that we are and dream to be. As Einstein observed, 'God is Love and Love is God.' My connection to God began when I was seven after a cluster of traumatic events; where when I prayed for the first time, I felt a warmth enfold me. This sense of the experience of the force of God became the organizing principle that brought me through some true horrors that otherwise would have broken me. In fact, I believe that God/Love is the key organizing principle in nature and of all life, and it is because we have become so disconnected from this force of intelligence and good that we find ourselves in the messes we get caught in.

Like nature, we are designed and wired with this God-force intelligence. It is our origin, our foundation, that pushes us to keep growing into the fullest expression of who we are. There is always a way forward, though it is not obvious at first glance until we look deeper.

Know this with certainty: no matter the challenges you may be facing, you are a powerhouse of potential and possibilities designed to meet any challenge and thrive. You are an unstoppable force of nature—millions of years in the making, with all the transformational power of creation and renewal at your fingertips. Acknowledging and accepting these facts initiates the new internal shifts of insight and awareness needed to reconnect with the innate richness and joyful aliveness you were born with. We all long to embody this richness, serving as the compass that aligns us with our fullest authentic nature and divine destiny.

Yet, despite this boundless potential, you may ask, why, then, do we often feel stuck and stagnant? Unconscious beliefs are the answer to that question. The common beliefs most of us share in silence are beliefs that whisper you aren't enough—whether not strong enough, smart enough, or creative enough—along with the fears of failure, ridicule, and not fitting in. All of these are pure fiction. But we believe them so wholeheartedly to our own detriment. Believing in this disordered inner chatter keeps us powerless, trapped in place. When we buy into these falsehoods, we cut ourselves off from the life we long to live and the gifts we are meant to share with the world. All loss is the result of scattered consciousness. All success is the result of clearly cultivated and directed consciousness.

Creating the Desired Change

But here's the good news: opening to the vast power and possibility of you begins when you stop believing in the fiction of these false beliefs and embrace the truth of who you are: a miracle of nature, capable of transforming your life at will. There is one key insight I would like to share that can spark new insight and momentum in your life—a mindset shift and practice that, when implemented daily, can shift the way you relate to your thoughts, emotions, and feelings, breaking free from the hidden habits and beliefs that drain your life force.

This insight transformed my life on countless levels. It removes all my possible excuses and any unconscious addiction to 'negative' emotional states when they arise, especially when fear and false beliefs infiltrate my thoughts.

Are you ready for it?

You Get to Keep What You Defend.

When you choose to keep defending your limitations, weaknesses, dysfunctional emotional states, and lack of power or action, you get to keep them. Whether these limitations stem from cultural, societal, or personal beliefs formed through environment or trauma, when we defend them, we hold onto them—or, more accurately, they hold us.

What we need to do is investigate, embark on the journey of knowing ourselves, and get in touch with these unconscious influences that perpetuate us, creating excuse after excuse to not follow through with our dreams, ushering them into reality. We need to meet the buried pain that causes confusion, self-doubt, and self-sabotage within us. This is a path of healing into our innate wholeness.

When I use the word "heal," I don't mean it as an abstract metaphor. Healing comes from the Latin word *integrare*, meaning to restore integrity and wholeness. Essentially, healing is about putting the pieces of our fragmented self together like a puzzle to remember and see a fuller picture of who we are.

Before we can affect any change or transformation, we must first be completely present with what is. To restore that wholeness, we must meet and feel the reality of the pain within us—the pain that has shaped the beliefs, habits, and patterns holding our true potential back. This is one crucial step in the process of personal discovery and evolution.

However, when we start to identify the deeper core of why we are the way we are, we often get stuck in cycles of pain and victimhood. We miss the next step that can lead us through and out of this stuck state. I've been there blaming and defending my right to hold onto anger, suffering, and my inability to take necessary actions to improve my life.

There's a valid reason why we do this, which I will explain later. It will remove any judgment and shed light on cultivating self-love and compassion.

When we are more committed to defending our vices and reasons for staying where we are than to defending our power and possibilities, we miss the next step. We need presence to meet what is and embark on the alchemical journey of transforming our pain into power and purpose.

One of my favorite quotes describes this process beautifully:

"The ore in the fire feels itself unfairly treated, but the pure gold looking back knows better."

This reveals another irrefutable truth: contrast and duality are essential forces that activate the alchemical process of transformation. Without them, nothing would exist or come into being.

Connecting the Dots: Wealth and the Rich Code

You may be wondering, what does all of this have to do with wealth and cracking the rich code? Life has shown me that true wealth comes from reaching deeply into life and ourselves, cracking through the surface of mere existence to the very depths of our souls. It's about knowing ourselves and fully embracing our duality and the dual nature of life. As we cultivate inner wealth, it is inevitable that it will influence all areas of our lives. As above, so below. As within so without. This catalyzing force creates the necessary pressure and friction for new creations to emerge. We are naturally born creators.

Consider this analogy: In a video game, we spend hours mastering one level to get to the next. Upon reaching that new level, we become beginners again at the next level, learning to navigate and adapt to the new challenges ahead. That's the nature of growth. As long as we are alive, we will continue learning, creating, adapting, and evolving—when we choose to, which is not always easy to do. Sometimes, it can feel like trying to pull a tooth when we are called to change something in our habits or patterns.

You might ask yourself, "Why? It should be easy to change if we know what to change. Why would we ever hold onto the habits, beliefs, and patterns that keep us from fulfilling our true nature and gifts?" The answer is safety. We prefer what is familiar over what is unknown, even if it holds us back. This is a trauma response.

Though we are wired to perpetually evolve, we are simultaneously wired to stay the same. I know, it's confusing, right? This is the constant pressure and rub of duality within us. This is where the rubber meets the road to catalyze new growth and transformation through the inner friction of two opposing realities within us.

We navigate two operating systems simultaneously: our biology—our nervous system and brain—and our soul, the ineffable essence of our authentic nature. Another reflection of our dual nature is that we have two brains: our limbic, primal survival brain and our frontal brain, where higher consciousness develops.

Our limbic brain is wired to survive. Its dominant mode is negative bias, meaning it always looks for what's wrong before what's right. This wiring has enabled our species to survive for millions of years. The limbic brain is much older than our frontal brain, which is why it always takes the lead unless we develop our frontal brain through willpower, self-discipline, and mastery of our thoughts and emotions. We then develop the skills to direct our thoughts, feelings, and emotions rather than being consumed and driven by them.

When we are triggered into our limbic brain, the frontal cortex shuts down—it has to. Just imagine what would happen in the wild if, upon noticing a tiger ready to attack, we stopped to consider which tree to climb instead of reacting instinctively. We would become the tiger's dinner.

The limbic brain doesn't differentiate between actual life-threatening events and imagined ones—like anxiety, which plagues a significant percentage of the population. Anxiety, usually triggered by past trauma imprints projected into the future, robs us of the present moment and the beauty of life. It robs us of our potential for sustainable love, joy, and happiness—the qualities that make being alive rich and meaningful.

More recent studies reveal that trauma is less about the experience itself and more about the impact and imprint it leaves behind. When love and support follow an experience, our nervous system can integrate and release the initial stress impact, much like animals in the wild that shake off the threat and return to normal.

When we're left alone in our pain, without support or a means to make sense of the experience, it festers in our nervous system, shielded by the numbed layers of our persona. When triggered, that's where the force originates. Whatever happened has touched something buried deep within us, causing us to defend and attack to protect that part of ourselves.

To experience the richness life has to offer, we must recognize and stop defending our unconscious habits, patterns, and triggers, allowing us to embody coherence and congruence with our soul. This alignment will enable us to build the life we long to live.

Until we identify and heal the trauma imprints in our nervous system, we cannot fully embody our soul gifts, purpose, and potential—those elements that lead us to a rich and fulfilling life.

You might say, "Oh, I didn't have any trauma," as many of my clients have claimed—as I once did, too—only to realize within the first hour that they indeed had trauma. Trauma exists on a spectrum; it's not solely about extremely harmful experiences, which is why we cannot compare traumas.

One of my favorite trauma analogies is: "Whether a bunny rabbit or a tiger chased you off a cliff, you fell and got broken in some way." The process of healing is the same, though the duration of healing varies. What may seem like a minor experience—such as being shamed or laughed at in school—can leave behind a trauma imprint, triggering a shutdown of an entire aspect of oneself.

Once a part of us shuts down, our nervous system does an incredible job of preventing the pain from resurfacing. It numbs us and builds layers of beliefs, ideas, and stories that become our new identity, deflecting and keeping the pain away. Our biology is also wired to seek pleasure and avoid pain, making it even harder to stretch beyond our comfort zones to implement change in our lives.

We tend to avoid confronting the pain that shaped our habits and beliefs. Instead of facing it directly, we often react defensively when someone comes close to touching this wound—a natural biological defense mechanism from our limbic brain. However, we cannot live a rich and fulfilling life if we remain trapped in survival mode, clinging to trauma patterns.

To heal the trauma at the root of these beliefs and habits, we need to rise higher—to a SoulSpective view of ourselves and life; gaining perspective from our Soul versus being caught in our story. We need to bring our heart and soul into the process of putting the puzzle pieces of ourselves together from the higher perspective of our frontal cortex, creating a coherent view of our existence. When we achieve coherence in our biology, our soul has the space to embody and inform us. This connection allows us to tap into the greater force of God/Good within us.

We must sincerely question what we're defending, with love and kindness toward ourselves, understanding the inner tug-of-war between our two operating systems. Are you defining yourself by just one piece of the puzzle? Are you even searching for the other pieces?

When this metaphor of puzzle pieces dawned on me, I visualized a partially completed puzzle frame with a center section attached by only a few pieces. I realized that I had spent years fighting and defending my limitations until I had put my pieces together enough to see a more complete rendition of myself. Those limitations reflected the outer pieces of the puzzle, which weren't connected to anything, yet I believed they formed the frame. I defined myself by the pieces I knew, unaware of the many more pieces within me waiting to be discovered.

When we are born, we are connected—we are pure expressions of joy, creativity, and natural intelligence—until life intervenes. Loss, abuse, grief, and conflict lead us to adopt beliefs that we are unlovable or that something is wrong with us, convincing us we are not, and never can be, enough.

Here is an excerpt from my book, *Resilience, Grace, and The Art of Showing Up*, describing the moment when we shift from our whole self to the beginnings of a fragmented self:

"It's about restoring innocence. The innocence that existed before our first pain. Before the first time we experienced the need to defend ourselves, or attack in defense. When the purity of Love of God/Creation flowed and lived through us, vitally and truly. As it does through every flower, tree, and blade of grass. To get behind and heal the shock and numbness we are all still in to some degree from that first experience of separation, violence, and hurt, and all the other moments that followed. Our reactions create layers upon layers of a self-created identity that lives separate from our original innocence and heart, our true nature. The journey we are on is to return to our original state of Grace. To return to joy and love and thus be governed, curious, loving, creative, kind, and playful."

This process requires vulnerability and an openness to the possibility that we haven't been seeing the full picture of ourselves or life. This vulnerability deepens our defenses, as it may require acknowledging that our interpretations might be wrong.

But what if we connected more deeply with the constant that exists beyond our limited persona and interpretations? What if we found safety there?

What if we sought to reconnect with and remember the universal frequencies of love, truth, and wisdom—the very forces that created us and continue to give us life?

What happens if, instead of defending our limitations, we begin to defend our birthright as sovereign souls? What if we embrace the innate power of the universe that lives within us, available in every moment? How might our life become rich in genuine love, joy, and fulfillment?

I know what happens: we come alive, and we thrive. My life is a testament to that fact.

When we heal trauma, our intelligence increases because we stop living from our limbic brain. Our frontal brain can activate, connecting us with that which is beyond our finite mind, linking us with the infinite potential within and without. This empowers us to reach for the life we long to live and make it happen.

The power and possibilities of you are infinite.

My message to you is that you are the miracle you have been waiting for, and you have the power to turn any challenge into an opportunity that grows your intelligence, love, and joy. Growth is a choice we make moment by moment, again and again. Letting go of the fiction, the false beliefs we have believed for far too long. Meeting the facts that trigger us, leaning into the friction and resistance we need to experience, is how we change. When we become friends with the facts that bring clarity—meeting the parts of ourselves we've been avoiding—our life changes, and we stop being stuck. We move forward rather than backward.

And yes, that clarity stings, which is why we often get defensive.

As the saying goes, the truth will set you free, but it will tick you off first.

These Universal Laws and facts are irrefutable and immutable; resisting them is futile and even harmful. These facts and truths exist to inform and empower us—to inspire new thoughts, awareness, actions, and choices. They remind us we are all connected, equally born with the power and capacity to influence and recreate our lives.

Our brain thrives on facts; it knows how to act when provided with clear information. However, our survival persona, mostly defined by fiction, resists them. When facts are softened to the point of being unrecognizable, our brain struggles to identify the next best step. Kind of like when there is excessive inflammation in the body, the brain-body communication system breaks down, and the natural stem cells our body creates to heal and repair get lost along the way. This brings us back to the truth: what we defend, we keep. When we keep defending instead of reflecting healing and evolving, we are robbing ourselves of embodying our soul, our authentic self, which carries the blueprint of our unique gifts to discover and bring to fruition.

Exploring and engaging in this process of knowing myself and healing has been my ultimate life's work. It has led me to richness in every area of my life that was once merely a dream—an enduring hope.

Whatever your greatest hope is, its realization lies on the other side of the triggers you defend, connected to buried pain that is ready and waiting to be healed. This may be the hardest path we can take in life initially, but it is definitely the most worthwhile, bringing riches beyond our wildest dreams.

It's time.

Time to love yourself so much that believing the fiction of fear and false beliefs is no longer an option.

You are worthy.

You are capable.

You are loveable.

You are enough.

You've absolutely got this!

***

To contact Luannah:

www.serenitybythesea.com or www.soulspectivesinstitute.com.

Bertie le Roux

Bertie le Roux is a transformation and leadership coach, keynote speaker, an author with over 40 years of experience empowering individuals, teams, and organizations to achieve breakthrough growth. He is known for his transformative approach to personal and professional leadership and love sharing his strategies for transcending self-doubt and fostering unshakable confidence. His insights always guide readers on a journey from invisibility to invincibility, drawing from both his personal resilience and extensive leadership experience.

A maverick and non-conformist at heart, his journey reflects his belief in possibility and perseverance. Told at 16 that a serious injury would end his athletic pursuits, he defied medical expectations to continue playing sports at all levels. This early challenge taught him that any goal is achievable with dedication and vision—principles that continue to inspire his clients and audiences worldwide. He has been honoured with multiple awards, including Global Influential Coaching Leader awards, and has spoken at premier events like the Global HRD Congress in Mumbai.

With 2 university degrees in finance/commerce and an education qualification, he has also served as a non-executive director on multiple boards and is a recipient of Rotary's highest honour, the Paul Harris Award, for service beyond self. Passionate about living a full life, he has travelled to over 40 countries, enjoys hiking, and remains active in sports. A devoted family man, he is married with 2 children and 3 grandchildren.

Belief to Achieve:

An Entrepreneur's Journey from Invisible to Invincible

By Bertie le Roux

In a fast-moving, results-driven world, success often seems like a mysterious formula cracked by a lucky few. Yet behind every high-achieving leader lies a journey—often paved with self-doubt, feelings of invisibility, and struggles for recognition. My path from being "invisible" to becoming a maverick, a change agent, and ultimately a beyonder has taught me that self-belief, vision, and resilience are not just ideals; they are essential for genuine transformation.

For most, the journey begins with invisibility—a state of feeling stuck, overlooked, or even questioning one's own value. Early in my career, I often felt my contributions went unnoticed, and I doubted my potential. However, I soon realized that invisibility is where growth begins. In those quiet moments, we find the chance to cultivate belief, define our purpose, and build a foundation for meaningful change.

Being aware of my starting point—a sense of invisibility—was critical for setting my future course. This awareness, alongside passion and purpose, shaped my journey. I've often found that the "road less travelled" leads to the most beautiful outcomes, much like my Hawaiian mountain hikes where the toughest trails offered the most breathtaking views. Trusting my judgment has enabled me to see opportunities others might miss.

Belief, the cornerstone of any transformative journey, demands resilience, especially when external validation is scarce. Procrastination in pursuit of perfection can be a hindrance, shackling our progress and fueling feelings of inadequacy. The desire to belong is natural, but true belonging comes at no cost to authenticity. For me, understanding my "Why"—the purpose behind my actions—was critical for moving from invisible to invincible.

Accepting my unique gifts, I walked away from people and situations where I didn't fit, knowing that my path was to stand out, not blend in. This self-knowledge has not only strengthened me but also empowered me to help others find their own "aha" moments.

I recall reading about a father who responded to his son's search for the perfect woman with, "Be the perfect man first." The same applies to leadership—true leaders must first understand themselves. As a Whole Brain Thinking Preference Practitioner, I encourage others to explore this deeply. The Neethling Brain Instruments™ (NBI) help reveal thinking preferences by categorizing the brain into four quadrants—Structured (L1), Detailed (L2), Creative (R1), and People-oriented (R2). This approach has been invaluable in my coaching practice, where understanding these dimensions has provided clarity on why we each do what we do, the way we do it.

In the business world, knowing our thinking preferences enhances communication, decision-making, and collaboration, enabling us to build teams that are aligned and effective. The NBI framework allows leaders to understand each team member's strengths, fostering a foundation for collective growth. Recognizing these differences doesn't only improve individual contribution; it strengthens the entire organization. Awareness of our unique strengths and preferences is foundational to managing relationships, leading teams, and making informed decisions, all of which are vital in becoming invincible.

Belief, however, is not arrogance; it is a quiet certainty about one's purpose. I am reminded of Steve Jobs' words: "The people who are crazy enough to think they can change the world are the ones who do." Self-belief, grounded in purpose, fuels greatness. True confidence doesn't shout; it knows the worth of its contribution even when unseen by others.

Vision is the bridge that carries us from invisibility to invincibility. I define vision as the "Imagined Reflection of Your Perceived Future." Vision isn't about planning every step but rather embracing the potential of what you can achieve. It serves as a North Star, guiding us through doubts and challenges. For an entrepreneur, community is a vital aspect of success. The relationships I've built within Rotary clubs, business forums, and even on social media have become sources of resilience and growth. Community support anchors a business, transforming it from an invisible entity to an invincible force.

A crucial but often overlooked aspect of success is community support, which helps elevate an entrepreneur from "invisible" to "invincible." No business can thrive without community. For me, actively engaging with local clubs, sports associations, and larger platforms like business forums and social media has been transformative. Community connections amplify growth, support you in challenges, and share your successes. The relationships I've built in these networks have provided essential support, anchoring my work in trust and shared values.

By investing in community, entrepreneurs contribute to a shared ecosystem where everyone benefits. Engaging meaningfully builds visibility, expands your brand, and reinforces the principle that no business succeeds alone. Positive interactions with the community foster a sense of connection, creating a support system that strengthens resilience and inspires others. As an entrepreneur, I encourage others to embrace these relationships, which aren't just for networking—they're vital sources of resilience and collective growth.

As I engaged more with community service projects, I became a more confident speaker and found my purpose as a thought leader. My fear of public speaking evolved into energy as the stage became my friend. This journey allowed me to step out of invisibility, fueled by the energy of those I served, and step into the role of an invincible leader for others.

While belief is personal, vision is something you can share to inspire and rally others around a common purpose. When I led Map Studio in South Africa, I envisioned a future where the company wasn't merely reactive to political shifts but positioned strategically to thrive through them. That vision, clear in my mind, enabled me to guide the team through bold, proactive changes that ultimately transformed the company's success trajectory. This experience taught me that leaders must carry a vision not only for themselves but for the entire organization.

However, as I learned, vision must be protected. Sharing it selectively helps safeguard it from detractors who may try to undermine your dreams. I've always advised emerging leaders to reveal only what is necessary to inspire, keeping their most vulnerable aspirations shielded from potential negativity. This cautious optimism allows your vision to grow stronger without interference from naysayers.

True transformation often requires defying conventional wisdom and stepping into the roles of a maverick and a beyonder. I consider myself fortunate to embody these identities. Early in my life, I observed that traditional leadership failed to empower those it purported to serve. Being a leader, to me, meant adding value, initiating change, and enabling others to reach their potential. During one negotiation, a director asked, "How do you get rid of the mavericks?" I was taken aback and replied, "Go on your knees and thank God for them—they're the ones who will take your company where it's never gone." It's about letting them loose to realize the untapped potential in your organization.

In my teaching career, for example, I quickly grew frustrated with the rigid, outdated systems that hindered real learning and growth. My success came from taking risks, challenging norms, and following an approach that prioritized impact over protocol. Ultimately, leaving teaching was an act of self-preservation, as it allowed me to step away from an environment that could not contain my vision or align with my purpose. This decision taught me that sometimes; to become invincible, we must have the courage to leave behind roles, people, or environments that limit our growth.

Taking Action: Practical Steps to Transform from Invisible to Invincible

1. **Cultivate Inner Belief**: Start by reinforcing your belief in yourself. In the face of doubt, focus on why you started, and use your vision as a guide. Techniques like visualization, journaling, or positive affirmations can be instrumental. Reflect on past successes, even small ones, to remind yourself of your capabilities. When I faced setbacks, I

reminded myself of past accomplishments, using them as a foundation for resilience and self-belief.
2. **Develop a Clear Vision**: Create a mental image of where you want to go, both in life and in business. This vision should be so compelling that it pulls you forward, even when circumstances are challenging. Ask yourself not only "What do I want to achieve?" but also "Why is this important to me?" A well-defined vision goes beyond traditional strategic planning. It demands imagination and an embrace of your future self, rather than simply reacting to present circumstances.
3. **Become Fearless and Trust Your Intuition**: Leadership often requires stepping into the unknown, trusting your gut, and acting with courage. I've found that some of my greatest successes came from trusting my instincts, even when logic seemed to dictate otherwise. Cultivate a relationship with your intuition—practice quiet reflection and pay attention to moments when you feel an unexplainable certainty. Trust that inner voice as a compass.
4. **Be Proactive, Not Reactive**: Invisibility often leads us to react to circumstances rather than shape them. To break this cycle, take deliberate steps to prepare for future possibilities. My strategic decisions at Map Studio were about more than addressing immediate issues; they were about positioning the company for the future. Avoid getting stuck in "crisis mode" and instead, focus on long-term solutions that align with your vision.
5. **Surround Yourself with Positive Influences**: Building resilience is easier when you have the right support. Seek mentors, allies, and role models who believe in you and your vision. A trusted network provides both guidance and accountability, ensuring that you don't lose sight of your goals during tough times. Remember that even when others cannot see your vision, they can support your journey to it.
6. **Commit to Lifelong Learning**: Leaders who are constantly learning can pivot more easily, adapt quickly, and inspire trust. Bill Gates, who reads voraciously, embodies this principle. Lifelong learning has kept me attuned to shifts in the business landscape and prepared me to tackle new

challenges with a fresh perspective. Whether through books, networking, or formal education, continuous learning is essential for maintaining relevance and resilience.

Reaching invincibility is not about being impervious to challenges—it's about shining as a lighthouse for others, guiding them through storms with confidence and clarity. The journey from invisibility to invincibility transforms you into a source of stability and inspiration for those around you. Much like a lighthouse, a leader stands firm against tides of uncertainty, illuminating paths not just for themselves but for others.

As you embrace this role, remember that invincibility comes from serving a purpose beyond oneself. An invincible leader is one who gives others the strength to believe in themselves, encouraging them to pursue visions they might otherwise abandon. In my career, I have witnessed the profound impact that one person's resilience can have on an entire team or organization. When you become a beacon of self-belief and vision, you give others the courage to reach for greatness, helping them to become visible in their own right.

To truly "crack the rich code," it is essential to rise from invisibility to invincibility by embracing belief, vision, and resilience. This journey is not just about reaching financial or professional success; it is about living a life of meaning and passion, one that uplifts others and inspires lasting change. The "richest" leaders know that real success comes from values in alignment with actions. Prosperity that lacks this alignment is hollow, but when purpose and action are fused, you create a legacy that lives on.

Embrace belief as your foundation, let your vision guide you forward, and take consistent action, even when no one is watching. The journey may begin with invisibility, but through resilience and clarity, you will emerge not only as a success story but as an invincible lighthouse, illuminating the path for those who follow.

***

To contact Bertie:

Discover more about Bertie's work at **https://www.bertieleroux.com** or connect with him on LinkedIn at **http://www.linkedin.com/in/bertieleroux** or simply scan the QR code.

Get Bertie's book "Belief to Achieve: A Leader's Journey from Invisible to Invincible"

Gayathri Riddhi

Gayathri Riddhi is a Master Certified Executive Coach and founder of Realize To Win, LLC, where she specializes in empowering leaders to thrive amidst disruption. With over 20 years of global leadership experience, Gayathri has developed a coaching approach that integrates deep behavioral insights with practical business acumen. Her diverse background spans industries such as technology, manufacturing, financial, health and professional services, where she has guided leaders from emerging talent to C-suite executives.

Gayathri's work is grounded in her strong academic foundation, including a Master's degree in Human Resources and her certification as a Master Coach from the International Coaching Federation (ICF). Her unique coaching model focuses on mindset transformation, blending mindfulness practices with leadership strategies to help leaders achieve peak performance while fostering emotional intelligence and resilience.

Throughout her career, Gayathri has led talent management and leadership initiatives that have had a significant impact on leadership bench strength, ensuring an equitable distribution of leadership opportunities within organizations. She has championed creating equitable and empowered environments, helping organizations build leadership pipelines that are both diverse and capable of driving long-term success.

Her coaching enables leaders to navigate complex challenges, align strategies with business objectives, and achieve sustainable growth. Gayathri empowers her clients to excel in their roles and create lasting, positive changes within their organizations by focusing on leadership transformation through mindset shifts.

Mindfully Shift to Winning Mindsets
Transform Your Leadership to Thrive in Uncertainty

By Gayathri Riddhi

Leading Through Disruption

Today's leaders face an ever-changing landscape marked by disruptions such as technological advancements, economic shifts, and global events such as pandemics or political instability. Disruption is inevitable, but how leaders respond to it defines their effectiveness. Leaders who possess a 'winning mindset' see disruption not just as a challenge but as an opportunity for growth, innovation, and reinvention.

Rather than being destabilized by disruption, these leaders embrace it as a catalyst for positive change, fundamentally shifting their leadership approaches, business models, and organizational cultures. The mindset they adopt during these turbulent times can determine whether they thrive or crumble under pressure.

The mindset of a leader ultimately defines their success. Leaders with the right mindset cultivate rich opportunities, relationships, and purposes, creating conditions where 'financial wealth' naturally follows. This is because they focus on 'mindful leadership,' remaining present, aware, and intentional in their actions, even during periods of turbulence. By leading mindfully, these leaders stay responsive rather than reactive, strategically pivoting to take advantage of opportunities presented by disruption.

Whether you are leading a global organization or a small team, the principles outlined in this chapter are universally applicable. Leadership is not about title or authority but about the mindsets that individuals carry. Winning mindsets ensure the leader's success and the success of those they lead, generating all forms of abundance.

The Mindset Transformation Framework

Mastering mindset shifts is key to thriving as a leader. The Mindset Transformation Framework, composed of the HALT, RISE, and

SHIFT frameworks, provides a structured way for leaders to identify toxic patterns, integrate mindfulness into their daily practices, and intentionally shift toward empowering mindsets.

These tools equip leaders with practical strategies for building rich relationships, identifying new opportunities, and aligning with their core purpose, which in turn leads to financial growth and other measures of success.

HALT: (Recognize Toxic Patterns)

The first step to transforming mindsets is gaining awareness. Leaders often fall into negative behavioral patterns, but these patterns can be recognized and interrupted using the HALT framework—Hesitation, Avoidance, Lack, and Tiredness. These four symptoms signal that a toxic mindset is at play:

Hesitation: Leaders who hesitate often fear failure or rejection. This stems from a 'scarcity mindset,' where mistakes are seen as threats to reputation or opportunity. The result is procrastination or delayed decisions, which stifles growth and innovation.

Avoidance: Avoiding difficult conversations or critical decisions is a hallmark of the 'victim mindset.' Leaders who feel powerless to affect change tend to avoid necessary risks, which leads to issues festering within teams.

Lack: The scarcity mindset manifests as a constant focus on what is lacking—resources, time, or support. This focus hinders problem-solving and creates a culture where opportunities are overlooked, preventing progress.

Tiredness: Emotional and mental fatigue are often signs of insecurity or over-control. Leaders who attempt to micromanage everything burn out quickly, reducing their ability to lead effectively. This exhaustion points to a deeper fear of inadequacy, which paralyzes leaders.

Practice Leads to Mastery!

Identifying these toxic patterns through regular self-reflection or team feedback is essential. Leaders can ask themselves questions like "What am I avoiding?" or "Where am I hesitating?" These questions reveal that hesitation, avoidance, lack, and tiredness are symptoms of deeper issues. Recognizing these signs is the first step toward transformation.

RISE: Integrate Mindfulness Daily

Mindfulness offers a proven way to recalibrate and reframe toxic thoughts and behaviors. By practicing mindfulness, leaders remain aware of their patterns, allowing them to shift away from toxic mindsets proactively. RISE—Routine, Intention, Senses, and Evaluation—gives leaders a set of practices to cultivate mindfulness:

Routine: Creating structured, intentional routines—like daily meditation, journaling, or mindful breathing—builds emotional stability and mental resilience. Leaders who start their day with mindfulness are better equipped to handle disruptions with clarity and calm.

Intention: Setting clear, mindful intentions each day acts as a guide for decision-making and interactions. For instance, a leader might set the intention to lead with openness and curiosity, which keeps them aligned with their values and vision.

Senses: Being present through sensory awareness helps leaders manage emotions and remain calm in high-pressure situations. Regular check-ins—like focusing on breathing or taking mindful pauses—keep leaders grounded.

Evaluation: At the end of the day, mindful leaders reflect on their decisions. Did they stay aligned with their intentions? Were there moments of reactivity? This self-evaluation improves future leadership and ensures they remain connected to their winning mindset.

Practice Leads to Mastery!

Implementing a 'Mindfulness Journal' allows leaders to record their daily routines, intentions, and reflections. Regular journaling reinforces mindfulness, making it easier to identify when a mindset shift is necessary.

SHIFT: Change to Winning Mindsets

After identifying toxic patterns and integrating mindfulness, the next step is shifting from limiting beliefs to empowering ones. The SHIFT framework—Stop, Highlight, Investigate, Flip, Track—provides a straightforward process for transforming mindsets:

Stop: Interrupt toxic thought patterns when they arise. For example, a leader who recognizes a scarcity mindset should pause to stop that cycle of fear and negativity.

Highlight: Once a toxic belief is identified, label it. Acknowledging the thought (e.g., "There isn't enough time" or "I'm afraid of losing control") brings it to light.

Investigate: Explore where the belief originated. Is it rooted in past experiences or assumptions? Leaders gain deeper insight by understanding their insecurities.

Flip: Reframe the limiting belief into an empowering one. Instead of "I don't have enough resources," shift to "I can find creative ways to maximize resources." This mindset shift opens the door to abundance.

Track: Tracking progress helps leaders solidify new thought patterns over time. Regular reflection on mindset shifts ensures that these new approaches become ingrained in the leader's identity.

Practice Leads to Mastery!

Include a 'Mindset Tracker' in your journal to document situations that trigger toxic mindsets, the steps taken to shift them, and the outcomes. Tracking shifts help leaders reinforce winning mindsets, leading to better decisions, stronger teams, and greater success.

Toxic Mindsets That Lead to Failure

Toxic mindsets not only undermine a leader's effectiveness but also erode trust and innovation within teams. Behaviors like territorialism, insecurity, and projection arise from these mindsets and create environments of fear and dysfunction. The three commonly observed toxic mindsets are 'scarcity, fixed, and victim':

The Scarcity Mindset

Leaders operating from a scarcity mindset believe resources and opportunities are limited, which fosters territorialism. This creates division among peers and discourages collaboration.

For example, a leader who micromanages their team due to fear of losing control stifles creativity and engagement. This toxic behavior limits the potential for individual and organizational growth.

The Fixed Mindset*

Leaders with a fixed mindset fear change, believing their abilities—and the abilities of their team—are static. This fear leads to territorialism and resistance to new ideas, ultimately stifling innovation.

Consider a leader who resists adopting new technology because they fear it will expose their lack of knowledge. This resistance frustrates the team and leads to broader failure that could have been avoided through adaptation.

The Victim Mindset

A leader with a victim mindset projects their insecurities onto others, avoiding accountability for mistakes. This fosters a blame culture, eroding trust within teams.

For instance, a leader who deflects responsibility when delivering bad news to the team damages their credibility and creates a culture of mistrust, weakening team cohesion and organizational effectiveness.

Recognizing these toxic mindsets is essential for leaders who want to create environments of success, trust, and growth.

Winning Mindsets That Lead to Success

Winning mindsets—growth, abundance, and resilience—help leaders eliminate toxic behaviors and foster environments of innovation and trust. These mindsets encourage collaboration, confidence, and accountability, enabling leaders to unlock new opportunities and achieve long-term success.

The Growth Mindset*

Growth-minded leaders believe abilities can be developed through effort, learning, and dedication. They see challenges as opportunities to grow and embrace vulnerability in the learning process.

For example, a leader who acknowledges and celebrates their team's growth after mistakes creates an environment of safety and engagement. This fosters long-term success through continuous learning and improvement.

The Abundance Mindset

Leaders with an abundance mindset view success as something to be shared. Rather than seeing resources as limited, they encourage collaboration across teams, empowering employees to step into leadership roles and work together.

For example, a leader who encourages collaboration rather than competition creates a culture of innovation, positioning the organization for long-term success.

The Resilience Mindset

Resilient leaders maintain a long-term vision, even in the face of adversity. They inspire teams to embrace change and focus on solutions, fostering an environment of adaptability.

For instance, a resilient leader facing industry disruption encourages innovation and problem-solving. By promoting problem-solving during disruptions, this leader ensures the organization remains competitive and innovative in the long term. This mindset helps the team thrive and keeps the organization on a path of sustainable success.

Shifting from Toxic to Winning Mindsets

Transforming toxic behaviors into winning mindsets is key to building successful teams and organizations. The HALT, RISE, and SHIFT frameworks empower leaders to eliminate territorialism, insecurity, and projection and replace them with behaviors that foster growth, collaboration, and resilience.

By recognizing toxic behaviors through HALT and cultivating mindful awareness using RISE, leaders prepare to shift their mindset. When SHIFT is applied, limiting beliefs are transformed into empowering ones. This process helps leaders adopt mindsets that drive success across all areas—personally, professionally, and financially.

Eliminating Toxic Traits and Mindsets

The three core toxic traits of territorialism, insecurity, and projection stem from scarcity, fixed, and victim mindsets. However, they can be systematically replaced with winning mindsets using the HALT, RISE, and SHIFT frameworks:

Territorialism (Scarcity Mindset → Abundance Mindset): Leaders with a scarcity mindset cling to control, fearing there isn't enough to go around. By shifting to an abundance mindset, they create collaborative environments where success is shared, unlocking creativity, growth, and opportunities for financial wealth. Teams working together generate more innovation and performance, leading to long-term prosperity.

Insecurity (Fixed Mindset → Growth Mindset): Leaders with a fixed mindset fear failure and resist risk, stifling team development. A growth mindset, however, views mistakes as learning opportunities. Encouraging experimentation and ownership allows teams to become more agile, boosting organizational adaptability and financial success.

Projection (Victim Mindset → Resilience Mindset): Leaders with a victim mindset deflect responsibility, eroding trust. Shifting to a resilience mindset, leaders take ownership of challenges and inspire their teams to stay focused on long-term goals, even during adversity. This mindset builds a proactive, solution-oriented culture that drives organizational and financial success by turning challenges into opportunities.

The combined application of HALT, RISE, and SHIFT leads to the elimination of these toxic traits and enables leaders to cultivate winning mindsets. This transformation generates not only successful teams but also long-term organizational growth.

The Impact of Mindfully Winning Mindsets

Leaders aren't defined by their titles but by the mindsets they adopt. Throughout this chapter, we have explored how toxic mindsets driven by territorialism, insecurity, and projection, hinder personal and organizational growth. On the other hand, winning mindsets—growth, abundance, and resilience—create environments where innovation, trust, and collaboration flourish.

The HALT, RISE, and SHIFT frameworks give leaders practical tools to eliminate toxic behaviors and adopt empowering growth-oriented mindsets. By integrating mindfulness into daily leadership practices, leaders can develop greater emotional awareness and foster resilience in their teams. This combination of mindfulness and mindset shifts paves the way for long-term, sustainable success.

Key Takeaways: The Power of Mindfully Winning Mindsets

Transforming Toxic Traits: Leaders who adopt a growth mindset leave behind insecurity, focusing instead on continuous improvement. The abundance mindset dismantles territorialism by fostering collaboration and shared success. A resilience mindset encourages accountability and forward-thinking, eliminating projection.

Creating Environments of Innovation and Trust: By shifting to winning mindsets, leaders build cultures of trust and engagement where teams feel empowered to innovate, take risks, and contribute to the organization's success.

Wealth as a Byproduct: Winning mindsets create conditions for financial, relational, and professional success. When leaders focus on growth, abundance, and resilience, wealth, in its broadest sense, becomes a natural byproduct. They can navigate disruptions, unlock new opportunities, and create lasting value.

Unlock Your Winning Mindsets

Leadership is not a static role, it's an ongoing journey of growth and transformation. The mindsets we adopt shape our decisions, the culture of our teams, and the potential for success within our organizations. By recognizing and eliminating toxic traits, embracing mindfulness, and shifting toward winning mindsets, leaders can profoundly impact both themselves and those they lead.

Reflect on your current leadership journey. Have you noticed patterns of territorialism, insecurity, or projection? Where do these traits show up in your decision-making?

How can you integrate mindfulness into your daily routine? Start by setting aside time each day to reflect on your intentions and align your actions with your core values.

Apply the HALT, RISE, and SHIFT frameworks today to proactively identify and reframe toxic behaviors into growth opportunities. Whether you lead a global organization or a small team, the power to transform your leadership lies in your ability to adopt winning mindsets.

This transformation is not just about personal success, it's about unlocking wealth in all forms: financial, relational, and professional. As you lead mindfully and cultivate winning mindsets, you'll inspire those around you to do the same, creating a ripple effect of success, innovation, and growth.

Are you ready to take the next step toward leadership excellence?

Leadership is a continuous journey of growth and transformation. Winning mindsets, whether in growth, abundance, or resilience—are what set apart leaders who thrive from those who stagnate. By focusing on mindfulness and shifting to winning mindsets, you unlock not only your potential but also wealth in all forms: financial, relational, and professional.

As a leadership coach with decades of experience, I've helped leaders at all levels navigate disruption and elevate their capabilities through a tailored approach. Whether you're an executive aiming to drive organizational success or an emerging leader stepping into a new role, my Leadership Coaching Programs provide a clear pathway to enhance your leadership potential.

What to expect:

Tailored One-on-One Coaching: Customized to your unique needs and challenges, ensuring maximum growth.

Strategic Leadership Programs: Designed to improve team cohesion, decision-making, and leadership presence.

Mindset Mastery: Dive deeper into adopting winning mindsets with strategies that directly translate into professional success and personal fulfillment.

Your journey toward leadership excellence begins with a shift in mindset. As you embrace growth, abundance, and resilience, you strengthen your leadership skills and unlock new possibilities for wealth, innovation, and success. The time to act is now. I invite you to take the first step in your transformation, aligning your leadership with the winning mindsets that will ensure your long-term success. Scan my QR Code below to learn more, schedule your consultation, and begin your transformation.

With purpose and clarity,

***

Gayathri Riddhi

Master Certified Executive Coach

Founder, Realize to Win, LLC

To contact Gayathri:

* Carol Dweck, "Mindset: The New Psychology of Success" [Dweck, Carol S. Mindset: The New Psychology of Success. Ballantine Books, 2007.]

Shafer Stedron, MD

Shafer Stedron, MD is a musician turned physician (Neurologist), Jay Shetty Certified Life Coach, Speaker, Author of children's book *The Boy and His Brightly Colored Blocks*, Founder of the children's literature-focused Little House of Dreams Publishing, and Host of the inspirational growth, health and healing-focused podcast Talks with Dr Shafer. Dr Shafer is passionate about helping others reclaim their stories and build their most beautiful future using her unique background in Neurology, Psychology, and creative arts. Dr Shafer believes that it is never too early to show young people how important their voice truly is, and the power they possess to create a better world, inspiring her work in children's literature and producing a children's literature-focused podcast, What's Up Young Authors! Approaching her coaching from a trauma-informed perspective, Dr Shafer helps clients realize that it is never too late to take back the pen and write your own story, even after long-term abuse or coping with chronic medical conditions. You can reach Dr Shafer on her website to learn how she can help you jump-start your journey to Mastering your Mindset with unique Neurologically-informed tools and a focus on storytelling to help you build your most beautiful future through 1:1 coaching. Dr Shafer has experience helping businesses unlock their team's full potential with her unique approach and can help you meet your goals.

Pruning: A Neurologist's Guide to Mastering Your Mindset
Begin to Build the Life You Truly Want

By Shafer Stedron

Success can feel too big to wrap your arms around. When examining the life of a person that is seen as successful, it can be hard to imagine how they accomplished so much. We put far greater emphasis on the achievement, and far too little attention is paid to the small, consistent, often painful steps and setbacks that it took to get to where they are now.

All we need to do to remind ourselves of the benefits of consistent, daily progress is to remember where we all started out in life: a defenseless mass of incredible potential, reliant on our environment and caregivers for our nutrition, warmth, safety, and mobility. Born with around 100 billion neurons, our brain needed a combination of appropriate nutrition and stimuli to help it start not only making important synaptic connections as we learned how to move and how to interact with the world, but also to prune back many existing synaptic connections. The very first example of the principle that more is not always better, and less is more. We needed to prune unnecessary connections to make way for important growth.

As our infant self, interacted with our world, our brains worked to tune out the noise and make sense of it all. At as early as four months old we learned about object permanence, the principle that something continues to exist even when we cannot see it. We learned how to read the expressions on people's faces to better understand our world. We mastered how to interact with our caregivers to remain safe and to get the love and nourishment we needed. We learned how to lift our head, then to sit up, then crawl, stand, and walk. We learned how to decipher the sounds around us into a language that helped us communicate our needs with greater accuracy and speed. We learned how to share, how to think critically, and how to start to survive in a challenging and exciting world with greater and greater independence.

As we get further and further out from the environment where we made so many fundamentally important physical and mental triumphs, going from a completely defenseless baby to a self-sufficient adult, our nervous system often starts to give us signals that something isn't right. Our nervous system uses the tools that it has to try to communicate to us that the way that we have historically approached the world in order to survive and have our needs met in childhood may no longer be serving us.

That pit in the depths of our stomach when we abandon what we want in an attempt to try to impress someone else. The fatigue we feel when exhausting ourselves to seek educational degrees and accolades, to participate in activities to show our goodness and worth and to accumulate wealth and external markers of success, when at the end of the day, we don't feel successful. We don't feel fulfilled. We feel tired. And we feel ourselves getting further and further away from our purpose.

When growing up our nervous system responded to the cues around us to form our habits and ways of interpersonally relating within our social structures (especially our family) so that we could remain safe and have our needs met. But if we grew up in an environment where the status quo was one that was not healthy, what feels normal to us may be far from it. Our brains seek to validate what we understand, expect, and believe. Because even if believing that we deserve better could lead to a better future for ourselves, it first requires that we accept that our past, the foundations of what made us who we are today, were built upon principles and beliefs that are not actually true. This requires a willingness to face our beliefs about ourselves and the world and question them. Questioning these foundational beliefs may feel like it threatens to topple the entire structure of who we are. Like a Jenga game, if we pull the wrong piece, the one lodged in tight, the whole tower could fall.

Many of us have formed a relationship with the world and our nervous systems based on beliefs that our safety is derived from getting the approval of others. Our early-life caregivers may have only given out love to us if we were performing to a certain degree or behaving in the way that they expected of us. While this may have kept us in their good graces as children, this blueprint for how relationships work is a set up in our adult relationships for a dangerous dynamic of power and control.

When we see our life as a story, as a book that we are writing, it becomes clear that when we look to external sources for validation of our worthiness and look to others to decide what we should do next, we are giving away the pen to our own story. We are in essence forgoing our opportunity to create the life that we want for ourselves. We are saying that someone else knows better what is good for us than we do.

This action is not a noble act. When we hand over our story, we victimize ourselves and all of those that we could positively affect when we lean into our true purpose. When we decide to live authentically.

Take a character cherished world-round as an example: Santa Claus. Can you imagine if someone had told Santa Claus that a fuzzy red suit with white lining and a black belt is a preposterous costume. How dare he dress like that? Any successful gentleman parading around the world should wear a suit! And a sleigh drawn by reindeer? Why Santa, don't you know that a Benz is a much more desirable ride? You are choosing elves to be your workforce? Well, you should really consider outsourcing. We are living in a post-industrial revolution, in fact! And watch it with cookies and milk, Santa. You want to slim down for the holiday season, that's what everyone expects!

Now I realize how ridiculous it may seem to bring up Santa Claus to help bring this idea to life. However, Santa's story is truly a perfect example of how your success is tied to your willingness to stay true to yourself, and to your ability to resist conforming at the cost of maintaining what makes you and what you have to offer unique. If you want to lead a successful and unique life, in tune with who you are and in line with what you want to bring into the world, you have to accept that you can only achieve this through leaning into your purpose. No one else can tell you who you are and what you want. No one else is responsible for you. And every time you abandon yourself to conform to the perceived expectations of others, you deprive yourself and the world of your uniqueness. You deprive yourself of the key to your success.

Santa couldn't have become Santa if he did not understand how to do the hard work to fully explore and embrace who he was and what he wanted to do.

When we see someone who is successful and so unapologetically themselves, it is easy and reflexive to think that they have it all figured out. That they are a person who naturally knows what they want and how to get it.

But the more likely answer to how people become truly successful, happy, and live a life in alignment with their true beliefs and values is that this person has learned how to question everything.

Not only how to question everything, but then how to question those hard-earned answers. And the next, and the next, on and on, until they distilled down the true essence of who they are and what they truly want from life.

They have learned how to tap into the ancient wisdom of their nervous system when it warns them that something is out of alignment. When the pit in their stomach turns, they don't cower or get furious with themselves, mistaking the feeling for fear or cowardice. They get curious. They say hello, sensation of fear. Hello anxiety. What are you trying to tell me?

Because when we are out in the world and making decisions about who we are and who we want to be, how we want to spend our time, and what legacy we want to create, we can only do so not by looking for the external validation of others, but by staying on course, heeding the cues our body gives us about when we are veering off.

As I said when we began this journey together, finding success can feel too big to wrap our arms around. But this is only true if we see success as something outside of us that we are reaching for.

Once we start to work with our body and with our nervous system to stay in alignment with our goals and our purpose, the feedback is clear, and the steps concise.

When we are starting from a place of dysregulation, we start the journey back to our calm and relaxed state one breath at a time. One breath in, deeply, holding it for four seconds, followed by one breath out, slowly, over six seconds. And we repeat, again and again, until we come down out of the ether of our fears and come back into our body. Into the here and now.

Once we are back in our body, focused on our breathing, on how our chest rises and falls, then we can start to take stock of the situation.

Are we in real physical danger? For this example, let's imagine that we are physically safe. We are in our home, surrounded by familiar items that we can use to ground us. We can close our eyes and zoom out, perceiving ourselves objectively as if we are a third party. I'm safe. I'm in my home, and my home is safe. The doors are locked. My neighborhood is safe. My city is safe. My country is safe. We can zoom out until we envision that we are looking down at the Earth from space, floating weightlessly in the black, endless void, staring down at a world that looks so different from above. Our problems and fears are no longer visible. They are too small, and they cannot compete with the grand vastness and potential of space. In awe of the simplicity, we see from up here, we can begin to bring ourselves back into our body. Back into our country, which is safe. Back into our city, which is safe. Back into our neighborhood, which is safe. And back into our home, which is safe. Now, we open our eyes, and feel our physical presence in this safe space, in our own body. We are no longer out of control of our body. We are back within it, having regulated our own nervous system, and trained our brain to be able to take a new perspective. To tune out the noise and the fear of what might be, and tune into what is in this moment, the safety and strength and mastery of our body.

Once we learn how to bring ourselves back into our body when we are feeling dysregulated, we can start the more challenging work of facing the triggers that lead to moments of dysregulation. I call this process the "trigger detector."

When looking for precious metal at the beach with a metal detector, sweeping back and forth carefully, you wouldn't freeze, drop the metal detector and run in the opposite direction if it went off, would you? Likely not. You would excitedly sweep over the area again, trying to close in on the treasure you have found.

Yet when we are navigating the beach of life and we feel those triggered feelings swell up within us we often get furious or fearful and retreat, freeze, fight, or fawn. When the threat is not a real, acute physical danger, however, we would be better served to get curious rather than furious about what triggers us. Because our triggers are most often clues to the patterns of responses that we formed in childhood to keep us safe as we navigated a world that was often out of our control. A world where we often had the least powerful position in the game. This may have been true at the time and may have served to keep us safe in the environment we were in (without a choice). However, now as adults we must recognize that the rules of the game have changed. We have agency. We have a choice in how we live, where we live, who we engage with, and who we walk away from.

So why are we still playing by the old rules?

Our brains seek out validation of the familiar. We hold our beliefs dear, whether they serve us or not. Until we are intentional about challenging our habits, our way of relating to others, and our beliefs about ourselves, they will continue to stay the same.

Like a hamster on a wheel, we will continue to run in the same direction, going nowhere, until we stop running. Because the body in motion stays in motion until it faces a counterforce. Until we challenge our beliefs, they will stay the same. Even the ones that no longer serve us and may be fencing us in, keeping us from our full potential.

We have to recognize where our behavior is taking us and decide if it is taking us in the direction that we want to go in, or if our responses are leading us off course out of nothing but habit.

To change the direction of our lives we have to stop.

Once we stop, with intention, and get curious about our triggers, then we can learn how to understand how we are showing up in the world. How are we making decisions, and how are those decisions impacting the course of our life? We can learn to identify the moments when we hand over the pen to our story, and how our nervous system warns us that we are once again veering off path. That we are in danger. Not physically in danger, but in real, catastrophic danger of losing our life. The life that matters. The life that is truly ours.

Once we learn how to listen to our nervous system, then we can get serious about the work of writing our own story. Of setting goals that get us one step closer to where we want to be. We have to go back to being an infant in our mindset, and this time, learn how to navigate the world in a way that helps us learn how to sit up on our own, then crawl, stand, walk, and finally, run. How to trust our "gut," the ancient wisdom of our nervous system, and lean into our fullest potential.

Once you start running in the direction that was meant for you without losing energy to external forces that have been fencing you in, holding you back, and wasting your precious time and energy, there is truly no limit to how far you can go. Once you set your mindset in the direction of your future, your potential is endless.

Let the pruning begin.

***

To connect with Dr. Shafer:

Connect with Dr Shafer on her website www.drshaferstedronova.com

Network with Dr Shafer on LinkedIn: http://linkedin.com/in/shafer-stedron-4b7a19263

Subscribe to Dr Shafer's Podcast **Talks with Dr Shafer** on Apple, Spotify, Youtube, and wherever you enjoy podcasts!

Follow Dr Shafer on Social Media as Talks with Dr Shafer on Instagram, Facebook, and TikTok

Learn more about Dr Shafer's efforts to help people recovering from abuse at www.wedonttellourstories.com and on Facebook at We Don't Tell Our Stories.

Learn more about Little House of Dreams Publishing on Facebook, and check out the What's Up Young Authors! Podcast on Spotify, Apple, Youtube, and where you enjoy podcasts!

Go to www.youtube.com/@TalkswithDrShafer to watch inspiring and informative episodes of Talks with Dr Shafer, from solo episodes that take you deep into the realm of developing self-awareness and reclaiming your story, to guest episodes where you will meet incredible people, hear their stories of overcoming life's challenges and the lessons they want to share with you.

Damian Nesser Ed.D.

A Life Design Coach, author, speaker, and educator of thirty years with a Doctorate in Education. Damian's experience with education was composed of being a schoolteacher, counselor, and dean. Born with Cerebral Palsy, he understands what it means to be an underdog and how to overcome, reinvent, and improve yourself. As an expert mentor, he and his team are sought after for their ability to draw out the best in their clients and develop the motivation to improve beyond what they believe possible.

From Struggles to Strength

By Damian Nesser Ed.D.

Miracle at Birth

In August of 1967, my parents, while on vacation in the Catskills, my mother's water broke! Within minutes, my father was furiously driving my mother for 4 hours back to Highland Hospital in Rochester, N.Y. The doctors stated it would be unlikely that I would survive being born two months premature. After several hours of uncertainty, my vital signs stabilized. The doctors also said I may not be able to walk, run, or play sports. I defied all the odds by being the captain of various basketball teams throughout elementary school.

As a result of being born with Cerebral Palsy as well as struggling in school with reading and math, I developed a tenacious work ethic that has stayed with me throughout my collegiate and professional careers.

With that said, I've reinvented myself three times in the professional realm: From branch manager trainee to classroom teacher; classroom teacher to school counselor; and school counselor to Life Design Coach. During the last two years of my mother's life, I worked as her full-time home healthcare aide. And while at times, life was incredibly hard and not knowing how I might survive financially, I reinvented myself as a Life Design Coach, paid speaker, podcaster, and mentor to my cohost of The Life Is A Classroom Podcast, Sam. I founded the Life Is A Classroom Foundation to honor my deceased parents Joseph, who passed away from cancer, and Celia, who passed away from vascular dementia. Recently, I was accepted into the "Who's Who In America", a global community of 1.5 million professionals.

A New Profession

My faith continually prodded me to suspend my life in Florida, move back to Pittsford, New York, and assist not only my mother but to relieve my brothers and their wives from accruing stress and anxiety because of Mom's declining physical mobility. My mother was diagnosed with vascular dementia and began facing the later stages of this chronic condition. Life can change suddenly and unpredictably.

For myself, life changed in a month. I made the decision to aid my beloved mother knowing it would be a daunting task. For the last eighteen years of my mom's life, my brothers lived in close proximity to her and were able to manage day to day tasks such as doctor appointments, visiting, and shopping for her after she had her knee operations. When mom had her knee replacements done, she began falling at home and later at the nursing/long-term care facility, I knew I had to stick with my decision to step up and take a leadership role.

I had no idea what awaited me in the world of vascular dementia. Questions, anxiety, and doubts all began to flood my mind: *How in the world do I take care of an 87-year-old woman who has vascular dementia? What is vascular dementia? Where do I begin? What would I do to survive financially?*

The time came for me to take the first step into a new profession and reinvent myself. I began by looking up the definition of "home healthcare aide" because I was unsure about the exact definition. As my research progressed, I became intimidated. The multitude of responsibilities including doctor appointments, administering medication, communication, and a plethora of other duties became a Goliath task in my mind. This fear which grew in my mind could either break me or make me.

When I first moved back to New York, I had to draw from my previous experiences: take off my dean hat, put on my counselor hat, and develop a plan of success for not only Mom but for myself as well. Thus began my journey of beginning a new profession as a home health care aide and reinventing myself into a certified life coach, author, and speaker.

"By failing to prepare, you are preparing to fail." -Benjamin Franklin

The Common Obstacles

Many people often face obstacles that prevent them from making the changes they feel are necessary to take control of and find a balance within their lives. These obstacles create apprehension but can also be a source of motivation.

One such obstacle is fear. There are many statistics regarding individuals who want to write a book: such a study was reported on in The New York Times stating that 81 percent of Americans want to write a book but less than 1 percent will write and publish a book. In the case of writing a book, it looks easy to most people at a glance but once they examine what is involved it becomes intimidating, and they give up. The reality is that fear has become an obstacle and prevented them from pursuing a passion.

Jessica Watson, the 16-year-old who sailed around the world by herself non-stop utilized a

Mark Twain quote in Part Two of her book: 'True Spirit' in which she states:

"Twenty years from now, you will be more disappointed by the things that you didn't do than by the ones you did do. So, throw off the bowlines. Sail away from the safe harbor. Catch the trade winds in your sails. Explore. Dream. Discover."

I mentored Sam from potential suicide to success. Sam came home one evening after a twenty-three-hour drive, sleep-deprived and unhappy with the state his life was in. The next day, in July 2016, he woke up in an Oklahoma hospital after doing something he never thought he would ever do. Sam awoke after attempting suicide. At first, Sam believed that he had only taken such drastic action because he was not in a clear state of mind. Sam thought, "After all, nobody in a healthy state of mind would want to take their own life," and he was truly convinced that he was not in an unhealthy state of mind. Sam is the type of person who tries to find the logical explanation for everything; the truth is that there is much more to it than simply being unhappy, stressed, or in an unclear state of mind. He simply had a talent for hiding his despondency, even from himself.

At this moment, he realized there were feelings that I was not addressing. It was not until nearly four years later that he began to understand how to express and manage these feelings. It wasn't until Sam worked in a Florida middle school four years ago and met Dr.

Damian Nesser that he gained the motivation and tools to improve himself and began to realize that, though it is important to acknowledge the struggles of others, it is equally important to acknowledge his own struggles and unhappiness. He began looking inward to see what was missing from his life, leaving him feeling unfulfilled. Sam also learned that it is not "selfish" to seek those things and take time to do things for his benefit. This contradicted the mentality that I held for nearly my entire life. I helped him become the catalyst for his own self-reflection.

Ultimately relationships failed as, at the time, Sam was still not very skilled at being open with others. But now Sam understood the things he was lacking to achieve personal happiness. Sam was ready to work on himself to achieve a sense of belonging and self-esteem and to find out who he was as an individual. Over the next four years, Dr. N. mentored Sam by providing opportunities to meet people who have overcome struggles, some similar and some vastly different.

Eventually, Sam returned to college with a different mindset and obtained a two-year associate in arts degree with hopes of transferring to a university for an undergraduate and/or graduate degree.

Thirty-one Years as An Educator

Currently, I'm employed as a school counselor at a middle school in Florida. I deal with a plethora of student issues ranging from anxiety, depression, teacher-student concerns, usual school paperwork, and, more importantly, navigating the world of student thoughts of suicide.

Coaching: Over the past three years, I was coached by Mitch Matthews, a Success Coach who I met online while at the initial Mastermind event of Amberly Lago, a Wellness influencer in September of 2021 in California. This was an amazing event because I met several successful women who came together to help each other learn, dream, and achieve to the next level. None of the ladies expected me to attend being the 'token male' in Amberly's words but, nonetheless, I attended, and wow, did my life change! I was inspired by the insight of 12 entrepreneurial women who have been encouraging me ever since on several social media platforms and other wellness events. The strategies I learned from the first unstoppable mastermind event have enabled me to have the courage to reinvent my life and overcome my fear of failure. My fear of failure stems from failing the 1st grade in Pittsford, N.Y. where my mother Celia, who owned a hair salon, was able to take time to help me in the classroom on a weekly basis pretending to be the classroom when really, she was watching how I progressed in school. I was very insecure going through elementary school trying to hone my skills in reading and math. I was in the low group, yes, they called it the low group back in the 70s for reading and math while my best friends on the basketball team were in the high group. They were just straight-up smarter than me! This educator is a tenacious worker who may not be the smartest, but I can and will outwork anyone.

Speaking: Over the past 31 years, I've spoken in and out of classroom settings to domestic and foreign audiences through my missionary work in countries all over the world. Flashing back to a funny story in 3rd grade with Mrs. Nathan. She couldn't shut me up on the reading carpet where we were supposed to sit and listen. Listening was a monumental task for me! Mrs. Nathan did one of the wisest things a teacher has ever done for me, she allowed me to teach the class and she sat in my seat on the carpet. It felt like the movie Trading Places. The class waited for me to continue the reading lesson by reading the book The Giving Tree. The class patiently waited for me to continue the story but the only thing I said was "Mrs. Nathan I'd like to sit back in my seat on the carpet". I never forgot that moment, not just because of the humiliation in front of my basketball teammates and best friends but something clicked! I began to realize how important it was to listen. It is truly an art, and it doesn't happen overnight.

Fast forward to September 2021 during Amberly's mastermind event, I was a guest on her True Grit and Grace Show (which is a top 1% worldwide podcast). The theme of my 10-minute interactive talk was how I learn, dream, and achieve in my classroom of life. I've been living this theme for 57 years and am continuing to make a positive impact on all walks of life. This journey has ranged from feeding homeless people on the streets of Bradenton, FL to networking in wellness events such as Secret Knock, (the #1 networking event worldwide) to sitting with and coaching CEOs, the discussions ranged from their company's mission statement, feedback on how their employees feel they are treated, headcount, growth, revenue projections, etc.

Training: in September of 2024, I became a certified member of the Jon Gordon Training Team. Interacting with his team on various occasions and studying and utilizing Jon's principles and framework has elevated my 'speaking toolbox' to the next level. In other words, we don't know what we don't know in life. Applying these principles within conversations has opened doors for booking speaking engagements for 2025. Learning from others who know more than you in certain aspects of life is a true joy. My dreams and goals are to have a positive influence in as many schools worldwide as possible. My plan which consists of my mantra is simple: learn from others who know more than me, dream by writing out a physical framework that can be accomplished by implementing what others have taught me along the way.

Author: If someone were to tell me then I would be an author someday I would have said, "You are nuts! An author? What does that mean? How do I even attempt to begin?" Through my Success Coach Mitch Matthews, I was introduced to Lise Cartwright from Australia. She facilitated and guided Sam and me from 'soup to nuts' on how to successfully complete a well-thought-out and purpose-driven book. There were a plethora of struggles and decisions that straight up stressed me out and I'm not a stress-filled person. It was flat-out tough at times. Sam and I learned so much through the process of becoming authors and now we're part of book #2, go figure. This counselor has gleaned valuable life principles from interacting with Jim Britt's group of successful, persevering entrepreneurs, and for that, I am extremely grateful. I am looking forward to seeing how this volume of Cracking the Rich Code will positively impact businesses, schools, churches, or even someone struggling to find their path in life.

Legacy: The Life Is a Classroom Foundation or LIAC Foundation was founded in November of 2021 in honor of my parents, Joe and Celia Nesser. To be frank, this is my heart of why I do what I do. Forming this nonprofit with my trusted coaching team members motivated me to branch out into the world of becoming a speaker, life design coach, and trainer to positively impact diverse student and or business organizations. I have such a burning desire to succeed in this endeavor so I can give back more to others. A good friend of mine once told me, "No matter how hard you work at something, there's someone out there who is working twice as hard as you think you are". You see my life's mantra is: learn dream and achieve to give back to someone who can't give back to you in your classroom of life! Giving back to someone who can't give back to me. This coach gleaned this principle from the great, legendary basketball coach John Wooden. This school counselor grew up playing basketball and it's the very thing that kept me motivated to continue to come to school. I probably would have dropped out if it wasn't for the influence of my amazing parents, who used to come and see me play basketball on Sunday afternoons after our family dinners. Family dinners? Is that becoming a thing of the past in America? My point for bringing that up is I've gleaned some fundamental, non-compromising principles from my parents which I then passed on to my students and clients to assist them in their time of need.

The LIAC Results: Over the past three years, the LIAC Foundation has had the honor and privilege of giving back to organizations such as:

- Take Stock in Children: Take Stock in Children was established in 1995 as a nonprofit organization in Florida that provides a unique opportunity for deserving, low-income youth to escape the cycle of poverty through education. They offer underserved students one-on-one support through caring volunteer mentors, professional college success services, the opportunity to earn a college scholarship, and hope for success in college, career, and life. Visit: takestockinchildren.org
- Feeding Empty Little Tummies (F.E.L.T.): Feeding Empty Little Tummies is dedicated to feeding Manatee County's most needy, homeless, and food-insecure students one backpack at a time. Visit: feltinc.org

- The Technology Student Association (TSA): This national organization of students engages in STEM (science, technology, engineering, and mathematics) There are engaging competitions for students to take part in across our great nation. Visit: tsaweb.org
- My local church: we gave back to 15 teenagers who enjoyed spending a weekend at a high school retreat camp, which focuses on developing their character as well as their faith.
- Sarasota, Florida: The U.S. Marine Corps reserve "Toys for Tots" program's mission is to collect new toys each year and distribute those toys as Christmas gifts to children in need in our local community. Their motto, 'Every child deserves a little Christmas' has been made possible thanks to their hundreds of volunteers. To see how you can support this program you can learn more here: Sarasota-fl.toysfortots.org/local-coordinator-sites/lco-sites/

Our Theme: 'For God so loved the world that He gave his only son so that whosoever believes in Him should not perish but have everlasting life.' – John 3:16-

***

To contact Dr. Nesser for coaching and speaking:

https://www.lifeisaclassroom.net

https://www.linkedin.com/in/dr-damian-nesser-27b35520b

https://www.facebook.com/damian.nesser.5?mibextid=LQQJ4d

www.tiktok.com/@dr.n.life.design.coach

https://www.instagram.com/dr.n.liac.podcast/

https://youtube.com/@dr.n.lifedesigncoach4044?si=CzEYQEUGP62t5A-R

LIAC Foundation

https://www.instagram.com/dr.n.liac.foundation/

Jean Yeap: Founder & Visionary Entrepreneur

Jean Yeap is the founder of the Katrin BJ Group of Companies and the creative mind behind the renowned brands La gourmet® and SHOGUN®. With over 30 years of entrepreneurial experience, Jean has built a legacy of innovation and ethical business practices in the Malaysian retail sector.

A graduate of the University of Malaya with a Bachelor of Economics, Jean gained international insights as a Commercial Officer at the Swedish Embassy, shaping her commitment to quality and sustainability. Under her leadership, Katrin BJ operates 35 specialty household stores, earning accolades like the Global Innovation Award from Chicago International Houseware Inc. and the Best Supplier Award from AEON.

Jean is a passionate advocate for sustainability and community engagement, collaborating with organizations like the Lion's Club and the National Autism Society of Malaysia to promote social responsibility. Her recent book, Unleash the Super Woman in You, explores themes of women's empowerment and wellness.

A sought-after speaker, Jean has addressed numerous conferences, including the Women Economic Forum and the AEON 1000 Suppliers Conference, emphasizing sustainable practices and inclusive education. Through La gourmet®, she champions healthy living and environmental responsibility, leaving a lasting impact on both local and global communities.

Frustration Led Me to Build a Business
The Birth of La gourmet®: Creating High-Quality, Affordable Cookware for Healthy Living

By Jean Yeap

From an early age, my passion for cooking blossomed, yet a persistent frustration lingered: the cookware available was either prohibitively expensive or made from materials that compromised health. Brands like AMC, Renaware, and Queens' Cookware offered quality, but their steep prices often felt out of reach. In contrast, cheaper options—like aluminum and carbon steel—were simply unacceptable for anyone serious about healthy cooking. After all, we eat every day; shouldn't we have a good quality pot to cook or stew our meat? Using a cheap quality pot to stew will inevitably leach out chemicals into the stew.

Fueled by a deep desire to bridge this gap, I took a leap of faith into the cookware industry. I sold my apartment—still under mortgage—and liquidated my MAS shares to gather the necessary capital. The journey was anything but smooth; I wore multiple hats as the business owner, administrator, salesperson, and even delivery driver. I had a business partner to help to co-drive the business.

When we embarked on this venture over thirty years ago, Malaysia's retail landscape was just beginning to take shape. Major players like AEON and Parkson were just starting their operations, and the government's push for modernization created fertile ground for our new brand. As we grew, hiring our first salespeople felt like a significant milestone, a testament to our determination.

But the 1990s brought unforeseen challenges. The Asian Financial Crisis hit, and the exchange rate skyrocketed from RM2.5 to RM5 per US dollar. Our reliance on imported goods made us particularly vulnerable. Our products were all imported so our business was badly affected. The whole economy in Malaysia was in turmoil. Our then Prime Minister, Dr. Mahathir intervened to peg the exchange rate at RM3.80.

The financial crisis hit our small company badly and we were juggling on how to pay bills as the business was in the 'Red'. I only knew I was resolute not to close the business so I resorted borrowing from family and friends to keep the business afloat, often making tough decisions in the face of adversity.

Though I held a degree in Economics, I quickly learned that academic qualifications could not prepare me for the harsh realities of entrepreneurship—especially during a crisis. Adaptability became my greatest asset as I took on increasing responsibilities and focused on understanding customer needs, laying the groundwork for a sustainable business.

To weather the financial storm, I looked for local sourcing and found a Taiwanese company manufacturing in Malaysia. They produce 5-ply 18/10 stainless steel cookware. This range together with our quality Classic range and Cook and Pour series of 18/10 stainless steel cookware elevated our brand and product range. As the economy stabilized, so did our fortunes. Retailers like AEON and Parkson opened more outlets, providing us with vital opportunities to reach quality-conscious customers eager to invest in premium cookware.

My early career training in Sweden instilled in me the importance of delivering exceptional quality and value. Quality and value become the standards we set for the brand of La gourmet®

Our brand evolved around two core principles:

1. **Healthy Living** – Crafting cookware that fosters nutritious cooking and promotes overall wellness.
2. **Conserve Energy** – Designing products that save time, energy, and costs while minimizing our carbon footprint.

These values resonated with customers seeking not just quality cookware but tools that empower them to create delicious, healthy meals for their families. Reflecting on my journey, the frustrations I faced earlier on became the catalyst for a successful brand that meets real market demands.

Today, whether in Malaysia or Singapore, nearly everyone recognizes and appreciates the La gourmet® name. This journey has imparted invaluable lessons, and I want to share three key takeaways:

1. **Passion is the Foundation of a Successful Brand.** A genuine passion for what you do, paired with a clear vision of how your brand serves its market, is essential.
2. **Personal Frustrations Reflect Unmet Needs.** By addressing your challenges, you may be solving problems for others too.
3. **Provide Value, Always.** Even if customers don't buy from you immediately, delivering value is key to building lasting relationships.

In the end, it was the journey through frustration that led me to build a brand that not only thrives but also enhances the lives of countless others.

Adapting to Change
Building a Resilient Brand through Innovation and Customer-Centric Solutions

As the business landscape evolves, particularly during the turbulent pre-COVID, during COVID, and post-COVID periods, it's crucial to acknowledge that customer needs and preferences are in constant flux. To thrive, we must remain vigilant, asking ourselves, "What new challenges are our consumers facing?" and "How can our brand adapt to provide effective solutions?" While our commitment to quality remains unwavering, our approach to addressing these needs must evolve.

In a world where time is a precious commodity, with social media, careers, family commitments, personal fitness, and sleep, all competing for our attention within that fixed 24 hours, the challenge becomes clear. Most will say "I have no time to cook, so I just 'grab', 'eat out' or do 'take aways'. How do we deliver nutritious, delicious cooking while also helping consumers reclaim their time.

The La gourmet® electrical pressure cooker is a prime example of our solution. It's designed to <u>save time</u> and <u>simplify meal preparation</u>, allowing users to cook with just <u>the push of a button</u>, freeing them from constant supervision.

Our evolution has led us to introduce cutting-edge small kitchen appliances that not only enhance the cooking experience but also minimize our carbon footprints. These "smart" kitchen tools empower consumers to multitask, enabling them to prepare meals reminiscent of home-cooked goodness—whether for singles, couples, or families. Busy career moms are relieved that they can have a career and yet able to cook for their family with these smart kitchen appliances that gives them "back time".

We advocate for cooking at least three to four times a week, particularly for singles and couples, to combat the rising cancer risks linked to excessive consumption of processed and fast foods—especially prevalent among younger generations. Research indicates that these dietary choices are significant contributors to health issues, and it is our mission to encourage healthier habits.

Staying abreast of new innovations to bring 'Newness' to the marketplace is essential for our brand. Without a continual influx of new products and ideas, we risk becoming irrelevant in a rapidly changing market. Our offerings must tackle contemporary challenges while delivering enjoyment and ease in the kitchen.

At La gourmet®, we believe that building a brand means actively listening to consumers and solving their problems. Our mission is to make cooking a joy, providing simple, user-friendly tools that empower individuals to take control of their ingredients and cooking methods. We wholeheartedly encourage home cooking, as it remains a straightforward solution for healthier eating and dietary control.

Our entrepreneurial journey has also led us to explore markets beyond our own, drawing inspiration from global trends. During my twenties, a visit to Lake District in the UK introduced me to Lakeland, a concept store that sparked our vision of creating specialty shops for kitchen enthusiasts. A later trip to Chicago revealed more inspiration in shops like Williams Sonoma, reinforcing our desire to establish a "Specialty Kitchen Shop."

These stores would serve as a one-stop destination for kitchen needs, featuring exclusive global brands and premium products.

Today we have 16 specialty shops, called "KITCHEN SHOP" with tagline, 'Pay Less For More'.

To further enhance the La gourmet® experience, we have established dedicated experience centers solely for our brand. These centers allow customers to explore our full range of cookware, participate in engaging cooking classes, and benefit from the expertise of knowledgeable sales consultants. To date, we have 5 La gourmet® Specialty Shops.

Apart from owning our own Specialty shops, we are also in all platforms namely:

1. Department Stores
2. Gourmet Supermarkets
3. Our own online platforms
4. Lazada and Shopee
5. KOL's platforms
6. M.D's Kitchen by Jean Yeap

Using these platforms and through innovation and a customer-centric approach, we aim to create a resilient brand that meets the evolving needs of our consumers while promoting healthier lifestyles.

Stay Focused

As entrepreneurs, we are always on the lookout for opportunities, keenly observing today's challenges and identifying what needs to be addressed. The moment we provide solutions to these problems, we open doors for business growth, enabling us to scale our current ventures. However, we must remember to **STAY FOCUSED** on our core mission. This focus is essential for our brand to become the best in the industry.

While opportunities abound, we cannot afford to dilute our attention or resources on ventures that stray from our core business.

The Importance Of Mentorship

As entrepreneurs, cultivating resilience, knowledge, skills, and motivation is crucial. From a young age, I understood the importance of learning from mentors who have navigated the complexities of business and distilled their insights into valuable books and seminars.

Attending relevant seminars has been a shortcut for me, fueling my growth in motivation, marketing, and resilience. Notable seminars, such as Jay Abraham's "How to Get from Where You Are to Where You Want to Be," Anthony Robbins' "Unleash Your Power Within," and Al Ries' "FOCUS" on strategic branding, have been transformative.

In today's information-rich environment, having mentors to guide us in business strategy, mental positivity, leadership skills, physical strength, and spirituality is invaluable. Building resilience, grit, and wisdom across these five areas can make you unstoppable.

Continuous learning is vital in our fast-paced marketplace. Recently, I have been exploring online marketing strategies and how AI can be leveraged to scale our businesses. Staying relevant requires us to embrace change and expand our skill sets with an open mind.

Seek mentors who align with your ambitions. Study their thought processes, successes, and failures. This exploration will help you carve your own path in business and self-discovery. Remember, the journey of learning is continuous; strive to be better than you were yesterday.

One of the most vital resources for developing our leadership skills is the practice of reading. Good books have the power to shape us and propel our growth. Here are some recommendations that have profoundly influenced my journey:

1. **Simon Sinek** — *Start with Why*
2. **Al Ries & Jack Trout** — *Focus, 22 Immutable Laws of Marketing*, and more
3. **Stephen Covey** — *Living the 7 Habits*
4. **Napoleon Hill** — *Think and Grow Rich*
5. **Jack Trout** — *Differentiate or Die, The Power of Simplicity*

6. **Jacky Tai** — *Get A Name*
7. **Al Ries** — *The Origin of Brands*
8. **Hector Garcia** — *Ikigai*
9. **Kahlil Gibran** — *The Prophet*
10. **Nelson Mandela** — *Long Walk to Freedom*
11. **Lee Kuan Yew** — *One Man's View of the World, From Third World to First, Hard Truths to Keep Singapore Going*

My inspiration in leadership comes from observing Mr. Lee Kuan Yew, the former Prime Minister of Singapore, and his successor, Mr. Lee Hsien Loong. Mr. Lee's foresight transformed Singapore from a Third World nation to a high-income economy. He understood that a strong nation requires an effective, anti-corrupt government and civil service.

Building a bilingual population with access to quality education and skill development was essential. Mr. Lee believed that a successful political system improves the standard of living for its people. He ensured affordable public housing and a conducive living environment. From reading his books and listening to his speeches, as well as firsthand experience with our company in Singapore over the past 20 years, I learned how he governed with justice and a genuine commitment to service.

Every Singaporean is provided equal opportunities for education and independence. Businesses are encouraged to flourish, and retirees are welcomed back into the workforce, supported with salary subsidies. This approach not only utilizes their invaluable experience but also reduces the burden on government resources especially on hospitality bills.

The Essence of "SERVICE" in Leadership

I realized and concluded that effective leadership is to use your skills and knowledge to service your key team to grow them, to motivate them to acquire skills and knowledge so in return they service their team of marketeers and sales teams. In turn, the sales team will educate our sales promoters on product knowledge sales techniques, merchandising, fostering motivation through rewards for achievements.

When promoters deliver exceptional service and knowledge to customers, inevitably customers are happy and will want to buy the company's products, fostering satisfaction and cultivating loyalty.

This cycle of service is when promoters deliver exceptional service and knowledge to customers, it cultivates loyalty and satisfaction. This cycle of service is how PM Lee transformed Singapore, a small island with limited resources, into a top-tier country known for its political and economic stability. He focused on nurturing people, providing them with opportunities, and helping them evolve into talents that propel the nation forward. The true treasure of Singapore lies in its people.

As a leader, we do the same and to recognise that our treasure is our people. Build our people will automatically build our brand and our company.

Building a Business beyond Products
Creating Lasting Value

Next, building a business is not merely about creating products; it's about generating **value**. It involves a constant inquiry: "How can I provide more value to my customers?" Competing on price alone is insufficient; the focus should be on offering the best solutions tailored to customer needs. This requires a deep understanding of who your customers are and what they seek.

At **La gourmet®**, we are committed to going beyond the traditional sales model of cookware. Our vision is to cultivate a vibrant community for those who love cooking or wish to learn. To this end, we have established cooking classes, workshops, and online resources, alongside a dedicated customer service team that prioritizes guiding our customers rather than merely selling to them.

Additionally, we are also proud to introduce our **"La gourmet® Recycle & Reward Program."** This initiative is close to my heart, as it embodies our commitment to sustainability. We encourage customers to return old cookware and small kitchen appliances to our stores, where we responsibly recycle or dispose of them in an eco-friendly manner. In return, customers receive rewards applicable to future purchases. We can also use old woks and casseroles to recycle as pots for our plants and herbs.

This program reflects our dedication to waste reduction and the promotion of a **circular economy**. It also strengthens our bond with customers, who appreciate that we are a brand that prioritizes more than just profits, we genuinely care about the planet. We are not just selling products; we are championing a lifestyle centered on sustainability and healthy living. We give talks to universities on sustainability, on global warming so they become more aware. Healing our planet starts with all of us.

We in La gourmet encourage harvesting our garden using organic soil. Soil is a limited natural resource that is vitally important to all life on land. There can be no life without soil.

The United Nations says that we have only about 45 years of Agriculture.

To us in La gourmet®, SOIL IS THE NEW GOLD. We as a community should start veggie gardens where we can share our produce so that we can be more secure when climatic change disrupts distribution and food is scarce in years to come. This is a start from your garden to a community garden so we can be self-sustaining and to be in control of the nutrients and organic veggies and fruits we consume.

As a leader we need to set the pace for our team leaders and rest of team to follow. Time is an essence, and all projects have to be delivered within the deadline with excellence. It is only with this mindset, together, as a team, as they will follow the pace that you have set.

In leadership I always train my team on 'Choices'. They can make the choice to be mediocre, the average or the best in all their undertakings. What they need to be aware is "The Sum of Choices they make each day becomes who they are!' Many of my team leaders are shocked as they did not realised or see the connection. I told them if you want to be in our team of talents to help me run this company, they need to make choice to be the best as I need "the best" to manage the process and to grow the company to be the best in the industry.

I open their mind that by making the best choices, these values will grow from mediocre to be the best as the original copy always stay with them.

During my meetings with the key managers, I always use only positive words of 'I CAN' and never 'I cannot'. I told them that positive words and mindset thinking is our everyday language as any challenges we meet can be overcome as "manmade problem, man can solve".

Beyond just 'service' as a living choice there is no substitute to living the Brand's Vision with consistency and high standards no matter what obstacles we encounter and to be ever so grateful with Love and Gratitude for the opportunities, the team, the products and the loyal customers that support our Brand.

As a brand we use La gourmet® as a platform to encourage customers on how we can do our bit to help Mother Earth. We hold sustainability talks, encourage family bonding using food and cooking as a tool.

Apart from caring for Mother Earth our brand cares for those suffering from Breast Cancer and heart diseases too.

Many asked, what? A cookware company? What can you do?

We understand from Pink Ribbon Wellness Foundation that the main cause of breast cancer is fast food and processed food… Food is the cause La gourmet® has the solutions to help cancer patients to use our Smart Kitchen appliances with easy and tasty recipes to encourage home cooking.

Of recent in 2024 we also got involved in the event held by National Heart Institute cum hospital as they also attribute Processed food as the main cause of heart disease. Similarly we in La gourmet® provided simple solutions to the heart patients that it is within their control as home cooking puts them 'In Control' of the foods ingredients they use and the oil they use for their frying Home cooking provides a healthier alternative and with the use of La gourmet® Smart kitchen appliances, cooking is easy to free their time to navigate other tasks on hand.

The Future of Entrepreneurship
Embracing Innovation While Staying True to Our Values

Looking ahead, the future of entrepreneurship is bright yet filled with challenges. Technology is evolving at an unprecedented pace, and the businesses that thrive will be those that effectively adapt to these changes. However, as we embrace new technologies, it is essential to remain grounded in our **core values**. Technology should serve our mission, not dictate it.

For **La gourmet®**, this means embracing innovations that not only enhance our products but also enrich the customers' experience. We remain steadfast in our commitment to promoting **healthy and sustainable living**, ensuring that our technological advancements align with our vision for a better future.

Vision for a Better World

As I reflect on the journey of **La gourmet®**, I see a brand that transcends mere products; it embodies a vision of a healthier, more sustainable future. Our mission is not just to provide exceptional cookware but to foster a community that values wellness and environmental responsibility.

The existence of a positive brand like La gourmet® can transform lives by promoting healthier cooking habits and inspiring a love for home-cooked meals. Through initiatives like the **"La gourmet® Recycle & Reward Program,"** we encourage responsible consumption while empowering customers to participate in the journey toward a greener planet. Each recycled item represents a step toward reducing waste and embracing a circular economy, reinforcing our commitment to the environment.

Moreover, as we continue to innovate and enhance our products, we aspire to create a ripple effect that extends far beyond our kitchenware. We envision a future where our brand nurtures creativity in cooking and fosters connections among individuals who share a passion for culinary arts. By offering classes and resources, we empower people to explore their culinary potential, enriching their lives and strengthening community bonds and family bonding.

Ultimately, La gourmet® is dedicated to being a force for good in the world. As we grow, we aim to inspire others to prioritize sustainability and health in their daily lives. Together, we can create a positive impact—one meal, one community, and one innovative product at a time. This vision fuels my passion for La gourmet®, and I wholeheartedly believe in its potential to contribute to a brighter, more harmonious world for generations to come.

Alone we can do so little.

Together, hand in hand, we can do so much.

***

To contact Jean:

 Scan to visit La gourmet Official Website

 Scan to visit MD's Kitchen by Jean Yeap

Georgene Summers

Georgene Summers is a born entrepreneur channeling a wild streak that just won't quit. Adventurer, author, motivational speaker, life coach, and inventor, the wildly animated Summers seems to have done it all.

Georgene spent several highly successful decades in the fashion accessories business between Los Angeles and New York City, followed by two years on Wall Street, before deciding to build a nightclub in the heart of Manhattan. Beyond trendy, Bolero hosted many hot, happening Celebrity-filled parties.

Not one to say no to challenges, Georgene then built a telecommunications company with 55 successful chat lines. Since 1996, she has experienced seven safaris alone, with no tours, in Africa, with only her Masai guide as company.

In 2002 Georgene moved alone to Africa, something that would change her life forever. Two years later she met her soulmate, a good-looking Brit. They married New Years Eve 2004.

Georgene, an accomplished Certified Strategic Intervention Life Coach, WHY Coach, Motivational Speaker, Author, and Inventor, has penned three informative books on relationships; her latest is entitled "Blind Spots: The Ultimate Guide to Love In The Dark." She recently completed her Memoir, "Angels In Sin, Mayhem, Money, and Murder," a page-turner that will be released in the fall of 2025. She is blessed with two little families she met in 1996 and 2002 while on safari in Kenya and put through school.

Fear, the Great Disabler!

Georgene Summers

It is no secret that we all go through life dealing with fear to some degree or another. Some fears are healthy and serve to protect you, while others are downright unrealistic, serving only to prevent you from living your dreams and reaching your highest potential for growth and greatness. Sadly, far too many people live their lives confined by the latter and are never able to jump off that proverbial cliff without a net and experience the thrill of facing fear head-on and winning.

If you look back and are totally candid with yourself, I am sure you will be able to recall numerous opportunities that you allowed to pass you by because of an unreasonable and perhaps irrational fear of the unknown. Yes, that place you failed to investigate but rather determined was too frightening, risky, and unknown for you to go there. Fear paralyzes us and prevents us from living our lives to the fullest and achieving our dreams, and yet we enable it to permeate our being on a regular basis.

I believe that in our lives, we can do *anything* we want or be *anyone* we want to be. What you need to have to accomplish this is passion and the motivation that comes with focus and determination.

There is no reason you cannot do anything you set your mind to, but passion and dedication *must* be present. I *never* say no to anything but rather follow the pathway of saying **yes** to all challenges and opportunities because the truth is you don't know if you can do something or not unless you jump in with both feet and give it your best efforts.

Back in the mid-80s, I needed a side hustle to pay for two rental properties I owned in Colorado that were not rented. I applied for a Showroom job making $1500 a month at the California Mart, which I thought would be easy to get as I had decades of experience in that field. For more than 20 years, I ran my own highly successful Fashion Accessories showroom there. It turned out I was wrong! The company that was hiring owned Duty-Free Shops in Hong

Kong, representing lines like Chanel, and thought, given my previous six-figure income, I was too experienced for the position.

I did not let that deter me. Instead, I bolstered the fact that they would be lucky to get me for such a knockdown price, and after numerous phone calls, they hired me. Three weeks into my employment, a large box arrived at the showroom, which I promptly opened. Inside were a series of handbags constructed of a very trendy, rubberized material.

Unfortunately, the bags while sleek in fabric were styled for "older ladies" like Boston bags and Hobo Bags. None of them related, style-wise, to the futuristic material they were made from.

Shortly after the box showed up, the owner arrived and excitedly asked me what I thought of the new handbag line. Without hesitation, I replied that it looked like it was designed by a blind person and that I could create a much better line. He called me into his office and asked me what I needed to accomplish the task. Now, unbeknownst to him, I didn't know the difference between a gusset and a grommet, but I stayed on course and went home to create the perfect handbag line.

Several weeks later, I returned with a large black portfolio and ten sketches of what I thought to be beautiful bags of snakeskin and lamb leather. He loved the line, but it took some convincing to get him to agree to the bonus I wanted and the fact that I insisted on going to Italy to oversee my creations. After a grueling hour and a half, he agreed, and a week later, I flew to Florence. The company contact met me at the airport and shepherded me to a local handbag manufacturing company.

Over the next day or so I selected snakeskin and leather materials, and the bag samples went from a dream into production. At one point the contact asked me if I wanted a gusset or a side or a bottom, to which I replied "I don't know" thinking he did.

The following day, I was presented with a beautiful line of one-dimensional leather and snakeskin envelopes. You could not get lipstick into any of them as they had no dimension. It didn't take me long to realize that the "blind person" who designed the handbags I had disparaged was my contact, and I had been sabotaged. He arrived at my hotel the following morning, and I led him into the lobby. I promptly gave him two choices: one; I would head home the next day without samples and tell the owner of the company what he had done. It goes without saying he would be very unhappy because they spent a great deal of money on the trip. Choice two: he could take me to the right handbag manufacturer, get the samples done, and I would say nothing.

He chose correctly, and I brought the samples back and proceeded to sell millions of dollars' worth of my newly created line to major department and specialty stores around the country. A few weeks later, the other partner asked me what title I would like to have. Without hesitation, I said, "Director of Design and Development."

I also got an override commission on the line from the dozen showrooms around the country that were selling it, so I ended up making $9000 - $10000 a month within the first eight weeks of my tenure. This was back in the mid-80s and was a very good salary then. Now, just imagine what would have happened if I had stayed silent and not staked my claim to designing a better, more saleable line of handbags. I would have been sitting in the showroom making $1500.00 a month! Which worked better?

So, I advocate this: SAY yes instead of no. You don't know if you can do something unless you get in there and do it. Now, maybe it won't work exactly right the first time, but you learn from your mistakes. When I hear people say, "I'll try," I immediately rise up and say try to pick up this pen from the desk. You don't try, you either do it or you don't. If you pick it up incorrectly and it falls to the floor, then pick it up a different way the next time and the time after that. Eventually, you will pick it up correctly. Each time you are not successful is a lesson in the classroom called life. You will learn what you did wrong and change it the next time.

The real challenge for most people is to push through the fear and risk, but you must. Without risk, there is no reward. Far too many people establish boundaries that they live within most of their lives. Now, loving and respecting one's family is a very important concept; however, denying yourself the freedom to soar like an eagle, to experience other cultures and countries, and to let these self-imposed boundaries prevent you from achieving is not acceptable.

That can occur when fear is passed down from generation to generation, which is all too common.

As luck would have it, I came from a family where fear was a large part of their narrative. This was partly due to my father being a customer's man on the floor of the New York Stock Exchange when it crashed in 1929, and he witnessed millionaires leaping from buildings or reduced to selling apples on street corners. Fear was a normal part of his life, and he often cautioned me not to invest in real estate or take a risk of any kind because of the embedded fear. Somehow, perhaps because of a left-over, rebellious attitude from my youth, I ignored the fearmongering and made my own path, meeting challenges head-on and jumping off the cliff without a net or anything resembling one. Because of that, I have had some incredible, mind-blowing experiences, and I urge my clients to be brave and fearless and step off the edge.

In a similar fashion, I believe that in the world of relationships, if it is broken and you can't fix it…NEXT! You have but one life, at least as far as we know, and there are over 8 billion people on the planet. Surely, there is someone out there who will love and respect you and support your goals and dreams. If not, you are better off alone than alone in a relationship. Trust me, there are plenty of people out there who are very alone, even though they are with another person. Frankly, there is nothing worse than that. At least alone, you can do what you want when you want and achieve the dreams that another person might not support.

In the late 70s, I separated from my second husband, and six years later, I made what I eventually learned was a life-changing decision. People often talk about things they have never experienced with a tone of authority that is unwarranted.

So, they "know" everything about China for example and would never go there, but have never even been there, so their "knowledge" is hearsay from the media or other similarly ill-informed people. When I moved alone to Africa in 2002, I had friends knowingly ask me why I was going to a place with Lions and Tigers and Bears. I had to tell them that there were no tigers or bears in Africa… but rather they were on another continent. I had been told by a variety of these people that the Firewalk was a fake. The coals were not red hot, and the entire thing was nothing more than a stunt if you will. Over the years, I have learned that one should not give a running commentary about things one has not experienced personally. It was interesting to note that when asked if they had done the Firewalk, been to China, or ever gone on a safari in Africa, the answer was normally a resounding no. So early on in life, I decided not to comment on things I had not experienced myself. It was on that note that I signed up for Tony Robbins Unleash The Power Within Firewalk. It was in the San Fernando Valley at a Sheraton Hotel, and it was in the mid-80s, so there were a few hundred participants, not a few thousand.

It started on a Friday night with several hours of seminar work that focused on healing the body from within, which was followed by the Firewalk. That was the start of what was to be a life-changing three-day event.

Since I was anxious to do the Firewalk, anything that stood between that and me was met with some impatience and a bit of annoyance, so the healing work we were doing seemed to be a bit of a waste of valuable Firewalking time. The Universe works in unusual ways, and contrary to my belief then, this work was to change my perceptions and my life forever. Around midnight, we made our way to the parking lot area where the pathways of red-hot coals stood, and people began to walk across them, albeit some with a modicum of hesitation.

I stood on the sidelines and argued with myself over whether I actually should walk barefoot over that path of burning red-hot embers. I reasoned that no one would know except me, but at the end of the day, I was the most important person anyway. Then I watched as two little people were aided across the coals, and I marched into line. I was several people back from the front, and the coals were getting darker, so that made me even happier. Just as I reached the front of the line, I heard someone say, "More hot coals," and a wheelbarrow arrived, and its' contents were dumped right in front of me.

I had no choice but to step off, repeating "cool moss" as instructed. By the time I reached the halfway mark, I could feel a burning on both of my insteps. I made my way to the wet grass at the end, and by that time, I had made up my mind not to return the following day for the seminar. Feeling very sorry for myself and in a degree of pain, I went back to the seminar to finish the night before heading home.

I arrived at my apartment at about 4:00 am, exhausted and feeling sorry for myself. It was a big mistake as I was about to learn a life-changing lesson. I pulled off my clothing and saw two fully formed clusters of blisters filled with liquid on each of my insteps, but I was far too tired to do anything about them. I put my socks back on and fell into bed, vowing to keep the hair appointment I had early the next morning but not to go back to the seminar.

I woke up a few hours later, took off my socks, and to my amazement, the blisters were totally healed and crusted over as if they had been there for weeks, not hours. I was in shock but soon realized that the work we had done earlier in the evening to heal our bodies from within had been effective. While I was also shown how real the Firewalk was, I learned how amazing the healing meditation had been. I couldn't wait to get to the seminar that morning and share my experience. I believe that changed my life and made me even more fearless, in a good way, than before.

It is all about change, changing your old beliefs into new, improved ones. It is not magic, but once it happens, it will seem magical. You take your old unrealistic, unwarranted fears and replace them with the courage and conviction to just say yes and go for it. You stop preventing yourself from limiting your life based on the fears that are within.

It is very important that you understand your values and what you truly want for your life, not just what sounds good. Far too many people ask for something in their life even though they have not thought it through. The Universe will provide you with what you desire if you focus on it and have the passion behind it, but often, one focuses on something that is not what they really want, and once they have achieved it, they realize too late that they were wrong. It is critical to look within and be honest with yourself about what your goals and dreams are on all fronts.

One client I coached stated emphatically that she wanted a friend-with-benefits relationship. Once she magnetized that friend into her life, it didn't take long before she demanded to know where he was and with whom. That clearly is not a friend-with-benefits relationship, so that was the end, but not without a lot of upset and unnecessary finger-pointing. That could have all been avoided if she had only been honest with herself.

This goes for everything in your life. You must be honest with YOU first. Look deep inside and ferret out your goals and dreams, focus on them, and make them happen. Do not be fearful of change, and do not be fearful of challenges.

Just jump in with both feet and do it. The worst thing that can happen is you have to do it again but in a different way. There is no such thing as failure. So-called failures are merely lessons in the classroom called life. You should use these opportunities to know what to change, what to do differently, and what to repeat. It is an amazing opportunity to learn and make your life the very best one that you can.

I have built many successful businesses just by jumping in with both feet and doing it. Businesses that I had never been in before, but I saw an opportunity and took it. Ten years ago, I went back to school to study to become a strategic intervention change coach with the renowned Tony Robbins. I also became a WHY coach, helping people find out what the right seat on the bus is for them so they could have a more fulfilling life. Think about the Manager of a busy store who spends her days dealing with customers and resolving their problems when her true passion is to be an author, sitting alone all day writing. She may complete her job, but inside, she is unhappy, stressed, angry, and impatient. This is why it is important to examine what your true calling is and how you can achieve it.

Each experience I have enriches my life as well as the lives of those I help move through the fears that are paralyzing them. Jumping in head-on to challenges has led my life in a somewhat unusual pathway. My safaris in four countries in Africa have blessed me with two families in Nairobi. They both found me on a social media platform over the past decade. One is my adopted daughter, who is a teacher now because I sponsored her high school. The other young man is a guide in the Masai Mara, and he and his wife pay it forward big time, getting running water for villagers who would normally put their lives in danger each day collecting water from the crocodile-infested rivers. My goal is to impact the lives of as many people as possible, and I can do that with my speaking engagements and my life-changing coaching.

***

To contact Georgene:

www.aworld4women.com

georgene@aworld4women.com

www.angelsinsin.com

Erica Gifford Mills

Erica Gifford Mills is an Empowerment Coach, International Speaker, Award-Winning Author, and Talk Radio Host. Founder of Balanced Symmetree, Erica assists busy women in opening their hearts, letting go of their pasts, and finding their passions to build and grow rooted lives.

As seen on Apple News and Google News, Erica was named one of the *2023 Top 10 Female Mindset & High-Performance Coaches Disrupting the Self-Help Industry*. In addition, MSN News included Erica in the *10 Visionary Entrepreneurs Driving the Future of Their Industries*.

Erica holds a double Masters in Human Resources and Management and is certified in life, business, and empowerment coaching through the use of integrative, holistic, and business leadership techniques.

Erica's signature coaching series, *The Rooted Life*, her live podcast, *Get Rooted Radio*, and her award-winning book and workbook, *The Rooted Life: Live, Love, Let Go*, teach women to be heard and to live it up, love it up, and let it go. She also volunteers locally and globally for women's collectives and the USO. Erica currently lives in Wisconsin.

Boundary Management:
The Foundation for Personal and Professional Growth

By Erica Gifford Mills

In today's fast-paced world, setting, communicating, and maintaining boundaries is paramount for personal and professional success. Boundaries, often invisible yet powerful, define our limits, needs, and values, protect our energy, and guide our interactions with others. Establishing healthy boundaries empowers us to prioritize our needs, reduce stress, and cultivate fulfilling relationships necessary for our physical, emotional, and mental well-being. This chapter delves into the world of boundary management, understanding boundaries, exploring their importance, practical strategies, and transformative impact on personal and professional growth.

Understanding Boundaries

Boundaries are the invisible lines we draw to protect our physical, emotional, and mental well-being. Boundary management concerns how we create, maintain, or change personal or professional boundaries to navigate the world around us effectively. There are several "types" of boundaries, including physical, emotional, time, sexual, intellectual, and material boundaries.

Boundary management theory suggests that we create, maintain, and change the boundaries we hold around specific roles to simplify and classify our situation and circumstances. They are the factors that outline our personal space, values, and limits of tolerance. By setting boundaries, we communicate our needs, preferences, and expectations to others. Setting boundaries is a form of self-care. It helps to create clear guidelines, rules, and limits on how one would like to be treated. They let others know what is and is not okay or acceptable. It honors our needs and wants so that we feel respected and safe.

Boundary management is essential and has its benefits if we know how to set boundaries. When boundaries are clear and respected, we experience greater autonomy, self-worth, and overall satisfaction. We must also learn that boundaries can and may need to be changed as we change and the lives around us change. What once was acceptable may no longer be acceptable.

I would like to give you some of my history with boundary management. My world began to falter when my beautiful, kind, and supportive mother was diagnosed with pancreatic cancer in October 2012. The prognosis was not good, and while we were still fighting it, we were also realistic. My father, my siblings, and I were preparing for her to die. She was not given much time, and even after having extensive surgery, the doctors believed she was living on borrowed time. My father took great pride in loving his family and was a fantastic husband. He was the type of man you looked up to not only because of his work ethic but also because he financially and emotionally supported his family and his love of life. The way he looked at my mother, you could see his love and adoration of her exude from his smile. My father, with a passion for his business but more so for his family, officially retired in January of 2013 at 81 to care for my mother and spend the remaining months by her side.

I received a call from my father in March of 2013 telling me the nurse wanted to speak to me. My first thought was of my mother. I could tell by his voice that something was wrong. A nurse got on the line and told me that my father had had an accident, and he would be transported to a hospital near me. I was stunned. He had slipped and fallen while walking the dog; he hit his head hard on the icy road, had bleeding on the brain, and was to have emergency brain surgery. This was not what I was expecting. He spent a few days in the neuro ICU after successful surgery. He was transferred to the inpatient rehabilitation wing of the hospital. He had an up-road battle of intense physical, occupational, and speech therapy. My family kept watch and made sure someone was always with him and then also back home with my mom, who was still going through chemotherapy appointments. After a week or so, he was doing very well, and his discharge date was moved up. Things were looking good.

It was a Tuesday night in March of 2013 as I was getting ready to leave the hospital when my father told me he loved me and he was so very proud of me. While I never wavered in my father's love and support, this came out of the blue. I asked him what he wanted and why he was buttering me up. We continued to get into our normal evening negotiations about what he wanted me to bring back to the hospital the next day. There was always a discussion of what time I should arrive, which I normally liked to get there for his first therapy session at 7 a.m. He, being stubborn and independent, did not like that so much. So, we entered our debates about when I was coming back in the morning and what I would bring him. After much discussion, we landed at 10 a.m. the next morning.

It was about 9:30 a.m. the following morning when I received a call from the hospital. There was a change in my father's condition, and I needed to get to the hospital soon. When I arrived, he was intubated, and CPR was being performed. I instantly went to his side, wiped his face, held his hand, and begged him to stay. I pleaded through tears of pain, sorrow, shock, and disgust that I had not been there earlier. It took about 15 minutes for me to get to the hospital, and it was another 20 long minutes since I had been there. With tears in my eyes, I told the staff to stop; I knew he was not coming back, and it was at that point I knew I had failed. No matter how much I wanted and needed him to stay, I could not save my father. I was devastated, and I still needed to tell my family. He was on my watch, and I failed them all.

My mother, who was a fighter, was still alive. She was kicking cancer's ass. She was sad, lonely, and heartbroken without my father. Because of the perceived failure of my father's death, I let this get the best of me. I was not going to allow another parent to die on my watch, so I kept an arm's length distance from my mother and did not speak to my siblings as I used to. I did not know how to set appropriate boundaries, and because of this, I lost precious time with my mother. Dementia started to set in; she was losing her memories and her knowledge of who we were until she died in December of 2018.

During the time after my father's death and between my mother's death, I met a handsome young man 9 years my junior. Things were good, and he made me laugh, which was something I had not done in a while. My son liked him, which was crucial and unusual. He brought joy into my life at a time when I needed laughter. Unfortunately, he had his issues, addiction. I thought this was my chance to help someone when I couldn't help my father. I was a fixer. I truly did not acknowledge this at the time, but because I believe in love and helping others, and my perceived failure surrounding my father's death, I wanted to help this young man and felt the need to help him. I was foolish, not weak, trying to solve what I could not. I thought I was strong enough to handle the darkest of places. I threw myself into a relationship that was not good for me. I wanted recovery for him and attempted to assist him for over three years to no avail. This might not be the way in today's world to be a fixer. It is unhealthy to love people who aren't good for you, to try to mend what can only be mended by that person. But I tried because it is inherent within me to care, want to help, and give someone chances to better themselves. I bent over backward, did things I would not normally do, and lost my boundary management and communication skills.

Near the end of this relationship, I faced a scare. In May of 2016, at the age of 42, I had an Ischemic Stroke. An ischemic stroke is usually caused by a blood clot that blocks a blood vessel in the brain. This keeps blood from flowing into the brain. Within minutes, brain cells begin to die. I was in the best physical condition of my adulthood, so I thought, how could this happen? I was training for a half marathon, eating properly, performing cardiovascular and weight training exercises, and, quite frankly, looked great. Unfortunately, the stress of the previous four years had taken its toll. Living with chronic, long-term stress is a contributing risk factor to having a stroke. The burden I put on myself by blaming myself and believing others blamed me for my father's death, burning the candle at both ends to help someone who would not help himself, not taking the time for myself, the guilt of missing time with my mother, and not practicing boundary management, all lead to this life-altering event.

I was doing better with boundary management. I truly learned my lesson and was thriving. Then, March of 2023 hit. I went in for my annual mammogram and was diagnosed with aggressive breast cancer. I immediately started chemotherapy and targeted treatment. Over the next 18 months, I had 20 rounds of chemotherapy and targeted treatment, five surgeries, including a double mastectomy, several blood infusions, and countless fluid treatments. I continued working because it made me feel normal. That is what I said anyway. It gave me something else to focus on, but I realized I didn't know how to change my boundaries. I did not want to ask, nor did I want to need help. I would review and answer emails on the days I had chemotherapy; on the days I did not, I would work until 5 p.m. I wanted to be a good employee; I wanted to please my boss and my staff. Perhaps I did not learn as much as I thought in previous years. Through those 18 months, I learned so much more about myself, gratitude, relationships, and boundaries.

When I thought I was returning to normal, the unthinkable happened. In September of 2024, two young Marines came to my home to inform me my son had died. My life was turned upside down. My son is my pride and joy, my sunshine. That sunshine was extinguished when he took his own life. While I am grateful to have had 24 years with him when I was not supposed to have him at all, I am still in shock and going through various stages of grief. I am trying to unpack all the emotions, questions, feelings, and everything else that comes with the death of the one person who meant more than anything to you. My boundaries, once again changing and shifting.

These stories are not for you to feel sorry for me. I did many of these things to myself. I was attempting to 'be all' to everyone. Hiding my true feelings, emotions, wants, and needs. I was taking on the responsibility of my father's death, my former boyfriend's addiction, my own guilt at keeping an arm's length distance from my mother and my siblings, trying to be the perfect mother, perfect employee, and showing people that I could 'do it all' and did not need help. I was not setting, communicating, and keeping boundaries. We must set, communicate, and keep boundaries to see their benefits.

The Importance and Benefits of Boundary Management

Boundary management is a crucial skill that can substantially impact our lives. When we fail to establish and maintain healthy boundaries, we may experience:

- Emotional Exhaustion: Overextending ourselves without setting limits can lead to burnout and emotional fatigue. In my case, serious health consequences.

- Resentment: Neglecting our own needs and desires can breed resentment towards ourselves and others. This is extremely common and often not even realized.

- Poor Relationships: Unclear boundaries can lead to misunderstandings, conflict, and damaged relationships.

- Decreased Productivity: When our personal and professional lives blend, focusing and achieving our goals becomes difficult.

Strong boundaries are not just about safeguarding our emotions and mental well-being or protecting our physical person; they are also a powerful tool for growth. By setting and maintaining healthy boundaries, we can:

- Improve Relationships: Clear boundaries foster healthier, more respectful relationships based on mutual understanding and respect.

- Enhance Self-Esteem: We can boost our self-confidence and self-worth by asserting our needs and values.

- Reduce Stress and Anxiety: Strong boundaries help us manage stress and anxiety by prioritizing our needs and limiting our commitments.

- Increase Productivity: Focusing on what matters most can make us more productive and efficient, especially in the workplace.

- Promote Well-being: Healthy boundaries contribute to well-being by protecting physical, emotional, and mental health.

Practical Strategies for Effective Boundary Management

As you could tell from my earlier story, I was not implementing boundaries, or, at the very least, I was not keeping my boundaries or understanding when to modify them. Although I knew boundary management was important, I lacked strategies and did not practice it regularly. Setting and maintaining healthy boundaries is an ongoing process that requires self-awareness, clear and effective communication, assertiveness, time management, digital detoxing, setting limits, and self-care.

- Self-awareness: Self-awareness is the first step in effective boundary management. Take time to reflect on your values, needs, and limits. Make sure you are honest with yourself. Identify your tendencies to overextend yourself or people-please and be mindful of these patterns. Set clear and achievable goals that align with your values and priorities.

- Clear Communication: Communicate your boundaries clearly and assertively. Use "I" statements to express your needs and feelings without blaming or accusing others. For example, instead of saying, "You always ask me to do everything," say, "I feel overwhelmed when I have too many tasks, so I need to prioritize my workload." Taking ownership of your feelings makes the other person less likely to be defensive.

- Assertiveness: Assertiveness is the ability to express your needs and desires in a direct and respectful manner. Practice active listening, empathy, and compromise to build strong and healthy relationships while still expressing your needs and desires, respectively. This also means listening to and acknowledging other's needs.

- Time Management: Effective time management is essential for setting and maintaining boundaries. Prioritize tasks, delegate when possible, and schedule time for relaxation and self-care just as you would schedule other important meetings, doctor's appointments, and events.

- Digital Detox: In today's digital age, it is crucial to set boundaries with technology, just as our parents did with the television. Establish specific times for checking emails and social media; leave devices out of the bedroom for better sleep and avoid bringing work-related devices into your personal space. Even set a few hours or even days to completely unplug.

- Setting Limits: Learn to say "no" when necessary. It is okay to decline invitations or requests that do not align with your priorities. It is also okay to decline because you do not want to attend an event. "No" is a full sentence.

- Self-Care: Prioritize self-care activities that nourish your mind, body, and soul. These may include exercise, meditation and mindfulness, hobbies, or spending time in nature. Self-care is not just the food you eat and the exercise you do; it is also what you watch and listen to and the people you spend time with.

These all seem self-explanatory; however, it is not always that easy. Setting and maintaining boundaries can be challenging, especially when dealing with people who may resist or violate them. There will be those who will be upset with you when you begin to set boundaries, especially when you communicate and keep them. They will see you as being stubborn, "changing," or being a different person. These are the takers. Stick to your values, needs, and wants. Here are some common challenges and strategies to overcome them:

- Fear of Rejection: Fear of rejection can prevent us from setting boundaries. Remember that setting boundaries is not selfish but a form of self-care and self-love. Those who do not allow this are not worth having in your life.

- People-Pleasing: People-pleasers often struggle to say "no" out of fear of disappointing others. Practice self-compassion and prioritize your own needs.

- Guilt and Shame: Feeling guilty or ashamed for setting boundaries is common. Remind yourself that it is okay to prioritize your well-being.

Many of the above challenges, namely fear of rejection, people-pleasing, guilt, and shame, come from a lack of self-worth and self-love. We want love; we want to make others happy. I understand that. Love the world but love yourself first. This world is sometimes dark and lonely and being open to giving and receiving love is critical, however, not at the cost of your heart, body, happiness, or peace. Do not allow yourself to be destroyed in the process of moving or not keeping boundaries. Know what you deserve, and never let yourself accept less than that. Healthy relationships start with mutual respect, and that includes respecting each other's boundaries. When that is no longer given, you must walk away, regardless of the relationship (personal or professional).

Personal and Professional Boundary Management

Boundary management is key when we are creating a work-life balance. Work-life balance is a term that makes sense to many of us but can be elusive to achieve. We all know the feeling when demands are piling up on one side of the work-life scale and dominating our days. Work-life balance is often used to describe a trade-off. You balance time at work versus time spent with family, friends, and personal interests. It can also refer to the level of flexibility team members feel they have. However, I do not feel it should be a trade-off. When we create the optimal work-life balance, all sides win. Boundary management is essential for that win. The workplace presents unique challenges for boundary management. Here are some strategies to maintain a healthy work-life balance:

- Set Clear Work Hours: Establish specific start and end times for your workday and stick to them. We all know that there may be times when a big project or a work trip requires shifting start and end times. These are exceptions and should not be the norm.

- Create a Dedicated Workspace: With the ever-growing trend of working from home or using remote work alternatives, having a designated workspace can help you mentally transition between work and personal life.

- Limit Work-Related Communication: Turn off work notifications during off-hours and avoid checking work emails or messages after the work hours you established above.

- Take Breaks/Days Off: Schedule regular breaks throughout the day to rest and recharge. Take vacation and personal time off. These are part of your benefits and salary. These breaks are needed to keep you productive and prevent burnout.

- Delegate Tasks: If possible, delegate tasks to colleagues or staff to reduce your workload. This does not mean you cannot complete a task on your own; it means you are spending your time wisely.

Healthy boundaries are essential for personal growth. We've already reviewed the benefits of boundary management earlier. As a reminder, by setting limits in our personal life, we can:

- Focus on Goals: When we protect our time and energy, we can focus on what truly matters. Allowing our children to see us set boundaries to achieve our goals teaches them to do the same.

- Build Stronger Relationships: Clear boundaries foster mutual respect and understanding in our relationships.

- Enhance Self-Esteem: By prioritizing our needs, we demonstrate to ourselves and others our self-worth and self-respect.

- Reduce Stress and Anxiety: Setting boundaries can help improve stress and promote overall well-being mentally, emotionally, and physically.

Conclusion

Boundary management is a critical skill for navigating life's complexities and a lifelong journey that requires ongoing effort and practice. Setting and maintaining healthy boundaries can protect our well-being, enhance our relationships, and help us achieve our goals. I told you a story at the beginning of this chapter because I forgot that boundary management needs practice and is a lifelong journey.

With boundaries, you can choose what you will tolerate and what you will not. You set limits on who enters your boundaries, what words enter your boundaries, and what stays out. Showing respect for yourself by setting and sticking with those boundaries is critical. If you don't, you risk your health and well-being. I hope you will learn from my experience. Remember, boundaries are not selfish but essential for our overall health and happiness. Setting boundaries is not about isolation or building walls; it is about creating space for ourselves to thrive. By embracing the power of boundary management, we can unlock our full potential and live a more fulfilling life.

***

To contact Erica:

International Empowerment Coach

Balanced Symmetree

Website: https://www.balancedsymmetree.com

Email: balancedsymmetree@gmail.com

Phone: +1 262.424.2548

Facebook: https://www.facebook.com/BalancedSymmetree;

Instagram: https://instagram.com/BalancedSymmetree

Twitter: https://twitter.com/BalncdSymmetree

LinkedIn: https://www.linkedin.com/in/erica-mills-76403a7

Lynette Weldon

Lynette Weldon, better known as The Caregiver's Coach, is a coach, entrepreneur, and frequent podcast guest who is known for delivering engaging, heartfelt conversations, empowering audiences to embrace their worth. Lynette is deeply committed to helping individuals unlock their potential and live with authenticity and purpose. Friends describe Lynette as the ultimate ally—compassionate yet tough, someone who will advocate for you fiercely while delivering the honest truths you need to grow.

Lynette's personal journey is one of resilience and transformation. As a mother of three, including a child with Down Syndrome and juvenile diabetes, losing her husband suicide, Lynette has faced adversity head-on while building multiple successful businesses, and is the founder of Lost Creek Ranch Camp Confidence, a 501 (C) horse rescue ranch that provides alternative therapy to youth and adults when traditional therapy doesn't work.

Her experiences have shaped her belief that true richness is not about wealth or status but about living with gratitude, authenticity, and alignment with one's purpose.

Through her coaching work, Lynette helps clients challenge limiting beliefs, embrace their worth, and find hope even in the hardest moments. She is passionate about guiding people to crack their own rich code, helping them realize that their past doesn't define their future. Her mission is simple, she believes that every individual possesses inherent worth and value.

The Courage to Live Authentically: A Journey to Purpose and Gratitude

By Lynette Weldon

I used to think that cracking the rich code was about wealth and status. When Jim asked me to write a chapter for the book I was honored! But my mind immediately went to "Me?" I haven't cracked the Rich Code, or have I?

Most people do not own multi-million-dollar companies or are independently wealthy. It got me thinking, we had a conversation, and he said exactly what I thought and felt. It really has nothing to do with money.

What do I believe it means?

I believe it has everything to do with how you live, feel and move through this world. I have always had a heart for helping people. I am the queen of second chances as my best friend would say. Sometimes to the detriment of my own well-being. But when I feel the richest, it is when I know I am making a difference in other people's lives.

I believe the first step is being honest with yourself. Being willing to be true to who you are and authentic. In our world today, it can be hard to feel good about ourselves somedays.

Just look at social media. Everyone is happy, beautiful, traveling. You see their fancy cars, expensive jewelry, and luxury homes. People start to believe everything they see and then start to question themselves, their situation and lives. Feeling like they are not good enough and then putting even higher demands on themselves. But we don't get the whole picture. No one is posting their bad days. No one is talking about how devastated they are because their relationship is failing, or their credit cards are maxed, or they may be so depressed it's hard for them to get out of bed.

I know for myself that I have suffered from imposter syndrome several times in my life. Even with my accomplishments throughout life, I never felt like it was enough.

I will never forget the moment I had to step on stage in front of hundreds of women, (women that I admired and wanted to be like!) to give a speech about how I had been successful that first year with the company. I was scared to death. Looking at all those same women, thinking this has to be a mistake, what could I possibly say that they would want to hear? They don't want to hear from me! The imposter syndrome hit me like a freight train, I wanted to exit stage left.

Then sometimes, it was a driving force to achieve more, but most often it was a crippling thought in the back of my mind. It was a feeling of "What if I am found out?" It wasn't until I was in my fifties that I started to really own who I was.

That's when I really started speaking my truth and feeling empowered. I stopped comparing myself to other people and their lives. I started to feel comfortable, really like who I was, what I could still accomplish and do. More than that, feeling empowered to share and be honest about who I am, past and all, to help other people. When we can be vulnerable, honest and authentic, that, I believe, is when we start to crack our personal rich code.

I think that there is a common thread today of wanting to feel "hope" We can't feel hope if everyone is portraying a perfect life. We can inspire and give hope to people when we are honest. When we are willing to be vulnerable and show our true selves. But being authentic isn't enough; it's also important to look at and challenge the beliefs that hold us back.

The second step: Being authentic led me to challenge beliefs

We grow up being told certain things from our family, church, school, the news and society. Throughout our lives we collect evidence on why that belief is true.

If I believed everything I was told throughout my lifetime, wow...I'd be doomed!

I think to grow and become better versions of ourselves, we need to pay attention to the tapes that play in our head and challenge our belief system. We need to ask ourselves questions.

Why do I believe this? Does everyone believe this way? Is there a different belief or way to look at this?

And those negative tapes that play in the back of our mind! Most of us are our own worst critics. Catching those thoughts can be difficult in the beginning. But when we start to realize what we are telling ourselves and challenge why we would think that way we can start to replace those thoughts.

Which brings me to affirmations. I am a huge believer in positive affirmations. I have them everywhere! Always have! We can't focus on both positive and negative; we must choose to focus on one or the other. When I am reading and seeing those throughout my day it's a reminder that I and only myself can decide how I am going to think and feel. I am the only one who can control my happiness.

I have been through a lot of challenging times and devasting circumstances that controlled how I felt. At one point in my life, I moved through life angry, frustrated and sad. I didn't like what was happening and I certainly did not like the fact I couldn't control it. (yes, I am a little bit of a control freak, but working on it...a work in progress!)

I needed to learn that no one was coming to save me. I was the only one that could change how I felt and lived. I couldn't continue the way I was and the only one that could change it was me. So, what was the next step?

Shifting my mindset wasn't just about determination- it was learning to see the good, every day, even in the hardest moments. That's where gratitude comes in.

Next step: Cultivating Gratitude

At least it was for me. If I wanted to change how I felt, I needed to start looking for the good things in my life. I was so focused on the problems I couldn't see all the blessings I had, even in the worst moments of my life, there were still blessings and an abundance of them.

When I look back now, it's so clear. Hindsight, right? I can honestly say that I truly am grateful for even the devasting things that have happened. Do I wish some of them would have been different? Yes. But what came out of them is incredible.

I have people in my life and relationships to this day that I wouldn't have had if those things hadn't happened. I saw incredible love and support; it gave me hope for a better tomorrow. I've been able to experience things in my life that I wouldn't have if things had been different. It shaped me and made me who I am today. It's shaped my children, their hearts, and who they are today.

When I think about those things, I am so blessed. When we feel blessed, we can't help but live from our heart.

I have a coaching program and one of the first things I do is ask them to start a gratitude journal. For a lot of them it's hard. They are starting from a place of sadness, depression and feeling no hope at all for a different tomorrow, The most common question I will get is "How can I be grateful when I am not happy?"

There are a million quotes out there on this, but I really believe and know it to be true, you are happy when you are grateful.

I ask all of them to just start with small things. A soft pillow, an extra hour of quiet, the phone call they got from their friend…anything that gave them a little happiness. They have to commit to doing it every day for thirty days. Usually at the end of that time, they see what a difference it has made in their daily life and how they feel.

It's how I start my day. There have been times when I have gotten so busy and don't take that time in the morning to do gratitude work, a few days later I will notice I feel a little different and have to ask myself what I stopped doing or changed, and that usually will be it, that is how much of a difference it makes for me.

Then came: Honesty

Whoa, that's been a hard one for me! Who wants to put it out there, all the mistakes and wrong or bad choices. But if we hide our past, mistakes we've made, how do we give people hope for a better tomorrow, a better future and really help anyone? I want to help people see that your past does not equal your future or where you can go, what you can accomplish or who you can become.

At any point you can decide to change things, to have a different life. To give it everything you have and go after and achieve what you dream, visualize.

I did a lot of things wrong. Some of them out of wanting to survive, some just because I wanted to do it my way and thought my way was best! Some just because I was defiant and strong willed.

I was emancipated and left home at 17, had my first child a few weeks before my 18th birthday. Not the way or in the order society thought I should. By the time I was 25 years old I had 3 children, finally agreed to marry my high school sweetheart, because the oldest was starting school and I didn't want to make it hard on him!

Obviously looking back on my choices, I took the hard road. But I never realized or looked at it that way. All I knew was that I was going to be successful and that failing was not an option.

Things were good, I had a great job and was about to have my third child. A beautiful girl (after two boys I had been looking forward to a girl!)

I was immediately told that they suspected something was wrong and a few days later confirmed she had Down Syndrome. That changed my whole world in a split second.

I will never forget that moment in the hospital, all I could do as the doctor told us the news was look at that beautiful little face and those big blue eyes and think, "What is life going to look like now? For you? Me? This isn't how it was supposed to happen"

Life was going to change for all of us.

There was no going back to life as I knew it. For years we were in and out of hospitals. She was diagnosed with a heart condition and then at 8 months old she was diagnosed with juvenile diabetes.

What I knew for myself was that I wanted to give my children and myself the best life I could possibly create for us. I was going to figure it out and was not going to be defeated or fail.

Mindset:

Like I said earlier, I was always determined to do things my way, stubborn and no one could tell me no. (My poor Mom)

I am not sure where my positive mindset came from. My Grandma was a huge influence in my life, and she always believed in me. My mother overcame huge obstacles in her life and was one of the hardest working women I know.

So, failing and not doing well in life was never an option for me nor one I would accept. I was ok with taking a risk, and never ever thought twice about it.

I went into sales and won my first car within 6 months. I didn't know it was supposed to be hard, until after I did it and was told most people don't accomplish that so fast or at all. I bought a coffee shop that was barely surviving and turned it into a successful coffee shop and restaurant. I started a horse ranch from a vision I had. I looked in the paper every week for the perfect location, never doubting that I would build it. It would become a reality. I had the mindset of succeeding, not wondering "if" I could, I just assumed I could.

I had a huge "Why" and stayed focused on that. My children were my 'Why", my driving force. Years later in a mastermind group a man I have huge respect for talked about your mindset, goals and the importance of having a "Why"

I had been doing this my entire life, I had no idea that's what I was doing!

I have a life coach I work with that. I believe everyone can benefit from coaching, no matter where you are in life. I adore this woman. She has helped me so much with overcoming imposter syndrome. She has drilled into my head that my life experiences and the things I have overcome are just as important and credible as the certificate or Ph.D. someone has hanging on their wall.

When you surround yourself with people who believe in you, lift you up, want to see you succeed, wow, things can start moving in a direction you never dreamed possible!

The importance of that is the difference in success and giving up. Sometimes it's the people closest to you, even family, that will be the negative ones. I think most often, that comes from love and wanting to protect you. Not wanting to see you disappointed or failing. But the whole point of life is going for it, at least that's what I believe. We can't win if we play small or play it safe. We can't make a difference in life or in other people's lives if we hold back and don't take a risk.

Finding Your Purpose:

For me, finding my purpose was the moment I truly felt like I cracked the rich code. Waking up every morning with a sense of excitement about what I could do, who I could help, how I could make a difference.

That feeling is like fuel for your soul. When you know what lights you up inside and gives you energy you can't wait to get up! Your purpose becomes the reason you jump out of bed!

But here's the thing, (or at least it was for me.) It is not always obvious. It doesn't always find you when you are ready. It snuck up on me in some of my messiest moments. Through challenges I didn't ask for, experiences I wasn't ready for and wouldn't have chosen given the option. Unbearable heartbreak, my husband's suicide, lessons I wasn't ready to learn. But looking back, those experiences shaped and molded me, for something bigger.

When I was young, I thought it had to be something grand, like curing a disease or a new invention. But what I've learned is that purpose doesn't have to be massive or life changing, sometimes it's quiet, it's in the way you love your family, show up for others, the way you use your gift to help others.

For me my purpose is deeply connected to helping others, whether it's through my coaching, sharing my story or just being there for somebody who feels like giving up. That's when I feel the most alive and connected to my purpose and so very rich.

One of the biggest lessons I have learned is that it's not about perfection, it's about progress. It's following and trusting those little nudges and whispers:

"What about this?"

"What if you did this?"

"What do you have to lose by trying?"

That's how it happened for me, trusting and acting on that little voice inside me, saying "Why not?"

And often, your purpose is hiding, in just a few questions:

"What makes you feel alive?"

"What could you do for hours and not notice the time go by?"

"What's something you've been through, that if you shared with others, would make a difference in their life and help them, give them hope?"

When you find your purpose, you find your power and when you find your power, nothing can stop you. Isn't that one of the richest feelings in the world?

Final Thoughts:

I am still learning and growing. I hope I never stop. But what I do know is that when I am living in my purpose, I feel rich, I know who I am and what I bring to the table. I am finally ok with it all, even the messy parts of my story.

Looking back on my journey, I realize that every challenge, every misstep, and every victory was leading me here—to a life that feels rich in every sense of the word. It's about the lessons learned, the people who've walked alongside me, and the moments when I've been able to make a difference in someone else's life.

My hope is that by sharing my story, you'll see that your past doesn't define you, your choices and how you move forward do. And at any moment, you can choose to change your story, step into your purpose, and create a life that feels truly meaningful.

It's built through every brave decision to be authentic, every time you challenge the voice of doubt, step out of your comfort zone and every moment you choose to embrace gratitude instead of fear. It's about finding your purpose and using it to create a life that lights you up every day.

So, what are you waiting for? Your past doesn't define you. Your circumstances don't limit you. You have everything you need to start cracking your own rich code right now, today.

***

To contact Lynette:

Lynetteweldon.com

You can also find her here:

https://www.facebook.com/coachingwithlynette

https://www.tiktok.com/@lynetteweldon

https://www.instagram.com/lynetteweldon3

https://www.linkedin.com/in/lynette-weldon-the-caregiver-s-coach

Join the private Facebook support group for daily tips and strategies at: Caregivers Journey to Joyful Balance

To book a free Breakthrough Session with Lynette: https://calendly.com/lynetteweldon

Sharon Hughes

Sharon Hughes is an award-winning author, speaker, coach, and host of *Called to Confidence podcast.* She is best known for her book *The Girl In The Garage: 3 Steps to Letting Go of Your Past*, where she shares her powerful journey of overcoming trauma and reclaiming her life. Sharon now uses her experiences to help women step into their God-given purpose by building emotional richness, confidence, and self-worth.

Her work has inspired women to break free from people-pleasing and imposter syndrome, stop second-guessing themselves, and embrace their full potential—whether in leadership, their careers, or everyday life. She believes emotional richness is the hidden key to success, helping others realize that what they believe about themselves determines the life they create.

As a coach, Sharon equips women with the tools to lead with courage and faith. Through her transformational coaching programs and courses like *Kingdom Confidence Method and Called to Confidence Course*, she helps women uncover the truth of who they are and boldly step into their calling.

Sharon is also a Police Officer Standard Training (P.O.S.T.) certified chaplain and a Critical Incident Stress Debriefer/Critical Incident Stress Manager (CISM/CISM). She lives in Southern California, where you can catch her petting every dog that crosses her path, eating an obscene amount of popcorn, and gazing at the sunset.

Emotional Richness: The Hidden Key To Success

By Sharon Hughes

When I was seventeen years old, my world fell apart. I was abandoned, homeless, and unsure how I would make it to the next day. Instead of high school, sleepovers and dreaming about prom, I was trying to figure out what to do next. Those days were full of heartbreak and uncertainty, but they also planted seeds of resilience I did not even know I had.

Fast forward twenty years, and I had built something incredible—an international home decor business, The Pansy Cottage and Garden (PCG), that received glowing press and brought me a level of recognition I never imagined possible back when I was trying to figure where to go and how to survive.

With PCG, I landed in two showrooms, had nearly thirty road reps and was on my way to success. I wanted to help others succeed so I started holding entrepreneurial events for women to encourage them to pursue their dreams. On the outside, it looked like I had it all. But the truth was, I was falling apart inside.

Despite all I had accomplished, I could not shake this nagging feeling that I did not deserve it. No amount of hard work was enough to silence my alcoholic father's voice in my head saying, "You're not good enough." It was exhausting and I felt like an imposter.

What I did not realize at the time was that success without emotional richness (ER) feels hollow. I have learned that true fulfillment does not come from what you have or even what you achieve, it comes from something much deeper. And that is what I want to share with you. This is not just an idea I have read about; it is what I have lived out. It is what changed my life and can change yours.

One morning, several years ago, I had a serious come-to-Jesus-moment when I was praying and feeling like I would not make it through another day. My life had fallen apart, and I felt absolutely hopeless. I heard God say to me, "What are you believing about yourself?" "Are you serious, you know everything" I replied. And he said, "Is it true?" No one had ever asked me that before. No one!

Those two questions changed the trajectory of my life and everything I believed about myself and the world around me. I call those questions, *"the God questions,"* and they are not just for me, they are for all of us. They are so powerful I have made them the foundation of everything I teach.

It is not easy to let go of the pain and beliefs that keep us stuck, but it is necessary to live an emotionally rich life. Why would you want an emotionally rich life anyway? Quite simply, there are things money cannot buy, like happiness and inner peace. Money is not the "be all, end all" despite what culture dictates to us. Hear me out on this.

How are you showing up for life?

I want to share with you what I experienced when I realized I was not alone in believing lies. I saw firsthand the weight so many people around me were carrying because they believed lies about themselves. They were successful, respected, even admired—but beneath the surface, they were each grappling with their own version of emotional emptiness despite outward success. How they showed up in the world illustrates what happens when we trade the truth about our value for the appearance of having it all together.

Here are three surprising interactions that shaped my perspective:

1. I sat in the conference room, preparing to lead a training on blind spots for the sales team in the $1 million club. This group was different from any I had worked with before. They had achieved many of their financial goals, and as part of the $1 million club, they were celebrated and given status by the company.

   But what I learned from this group underscored why ER is so vital. One of them confided that they went home to a lonely house each night. His wife had left him, and his children were not speaking to him. A stark contrast to the picture-perfect success he presented on the outside. Behind the polished exterior was someone breaking wide open inside, feeling utterly emotionally bankrupt.

What brought him to this place was chasing the never-ending-deals. Once closed, there would be the next deal, and the next. Always kicking the emotional bank account into the future and never making any deposits for his family to withdraw from. He felt defeated.

2. I could hear her footsteps echoing down the hall, everyone in the office knew when she was worked up, she had a reputation for storming through the office. She stopped at my desk. "I need to talk to you. Can you come with me?" she asked sharply. I nodded and followed her wondering what got her so worked up this time. Her gray-blue eyes were intense and looked like she was about to burst into tears. "Are you after my job?" she blurted out.

I was stunned and completely caught off guard, nothing could be further from the truth. Before I could respond, she waved her hand dismissively. "Never mind," she snapped and marched off. The next morning, when I got to the office, there was a cup of my favorite coffee waiting on my desk with a scribbled apology on a Post-it note. It was her way of making peace without having to say the words.

This was not the first time she had caved to her fears, blew up and then offered me an olive branch. I could see the cracks in her armor: fear, insecurity, and the deep ache of not feeling good enough. She was terrified that someone would find out she was not everything she pretended to be, and her career and status might be on the line.

3. He sat across from me, declaring with conviction that he liked himself, liked who he was, and had no intention of changing for anyone. But beneath his words, I could see the anger and fear he was trying to hide. That's the point, I thought, you should not have to change for anyone else. You should only change for yourself, because <u>you want to be the best version of you</u>, not to placate others or gain any kind of

approval. You are the only one that faces you in the mirror and you have to live with yourself.

Despite his confident assertions, I was not convinced. I saw through the mask he wore every day, the one he hoped no one would see past. The trips, the dinners, the designer clothes, the status; they were all distractions, covering up a deep emptiness and pain he could not escape.

What do these three people have in common? They are all fighting the same battle—trying to keep their humanity hidden behind their success and status. But here is the thing: the mask cracks and breaks eventually. No one can keep up the facade forever. Deep down, we are all just longing to be seen, heard, and fit it. We are human; after all, we are meant to belong, we are created for a purpose.

I cannot help but wonder who these three are behind closed doors when no one else is around. What do they see when they look in the mirror? If you see any part of yourself in them, or in my story, you are in the right place.

So how do you gain ER and stop wearing the success and status mask? It is the easiest hard thing you will ever do. These are the three key steps that helped me move forward, let go of the lies from my past, and embrace the fullness of emotional richness. These steps are not just concepts; they are actions anyone can take, no matter where they are starting from.

Step 1: Your Power to Choose

The first thing you need to understand to have a breakthrough is you have the power to choose, also known as free will. Why is this a big deal you ask? Because if you will not accept that you have the power to choose and use it to change your life, and what you believe about yourself, nothing will ever change for you.

This is the foundational piece to change everything about you and your life. You get to choose pretty much everything with very few exceptions.

Having the power to choose means you are in complete control of the choices you make every single day, all day long. Sounds good right? With it comes hard work because you must change your habits by making good choices if you want results. You cannot allow old patterns and old choices to control you anymore. I pinky-promise-swear this is the only way I know to get free from the garbage you do not want anymore. You get to choose to take out the trash!

Step 2: What You Believe Will Change Your Life

What you believe shapes your life, there is absolutely no doubt about it and tons of research to support that concept. The challenge is in believing what really is true. Truth is powerful, pivotal, confrontational, and critical to your personal development and living in emotional richness.

When I refer to believing the truth, I am not talking about a Pollyanna type of belief (unrealistic) but instead the belief that gives hope, purpose, joy, and yes, the will to keep moving forward when you feel like you cannot go on any further.

It was not until I started really digging into research on the power of mindsets, neuroscience, and the ability to create new neural pathways (how your brain stores information) that I understood how transformational our beliefs are. But with belief comes choosing what to believe. For example, have you ever believed something to be true and later found out it was not? The promise, the apology, the vow, the commitment was not true. And when you found out, even in the face of that newly found evidence, you chose not to believe it, but to live in denial? It is a painful place to be and has consequences.

Recently during a podcast interview, the host said I am famous for saying, "Believing a lie is just as powerful as believing the truth." I wrote that statement in my book, *The Girl in The Garage: 3 Steps To Letting Go Of Your Past* and I share it whenever I speak in hope it will cause anyone that hears it to stop-dead-in-their-tracks and evaluate what they believe.

I would not be doing my job if I did not ask you what you believe about yourself and if it is the truth. Take a moment to think about what painful lies you might be dragging around from your past. I have a hunch you may have something you believe that is not true, most people do.

Step 3: Who Would You Be If You Were Not That?

Who would you be if you were not the lie/label/thing you have been carrying with you? This is both a freeing and confrontational moment for anyone standing at the crossroads. I believed I was the girl in the garage, the throw away, unwanted, unloved, and abandoned. I had to come to terms with who I am if I did not believe the lies about myself anymore.

You would think this would be the easy part, but it is not. This is hard internal work. You might find it hard to figure out who you are now that you are letting go of lies and that is completely normal. A few years ago, I used these three steps in corporate training and a woman in the front row blurted out, "Free!" when I asked, "Who would you be if you let go of the lies?" Another time I used the same question with a team of professionals who were addressing how to overcome mental blocks that keep them stuck and two people started crying.

Make no mistake, this is powerful; this can set you free. You may not have any idea of who you will be, but free is an incredibly beautiful place to start.

If you find yourself thinking this all sounds like personal development or something to discuss in group therapy, you are not too far off, but there is a difference. Here are a few examples of how ER is different than personal development:

1. **Emotional Richness is a State of Being; Personal Development is a Process:** Personal development involves intentional actions and efforts to grow skills, knowledge, and abilities, whether it is improving leadership, communication, or habits. ER, on the other hand, is the emotional depth and fulfillment one gains along that journey. You can develop yourself personally without necessarily cultivating ER, which often requires a deeper connection to self and others.

   Example: Someone may work on time management and productivity (personal development), but without ER, like empathy, gratitude, or self-awareness, they might achieve goals while still feeling unfulfilled (this is what I saw in my supervisor that thought I was after her job).

2. **Personal Development is Goal-Oriented; ER is Purpose-Oriented:**
   Personal development often focuses on specific, measurable goals (e.g., career advancement, improving public speaking). ER, however, is about cultivating a sense of purpose, emotional well-being, and deepening connections to others and one's faith. It is less about reaching milestones and more about experiencing life in a full, emotionally aware way.

   Example: A person may pursue personal development to become more successful in business, but emotional richness allows them to find purpose and meaning in their work, beyond just financial rewards or achievements (this is what I saw with the gentleman in the $1 million dollar club).

3. **Personal Development Can Be External; ER is Internal:**
   While personal development can involve external factors—like learning new skills, acquiring knowledge, or achieving external success—ER is an internal state. It is about cultivating inner joy, emotional balance, and spiritual grounding that may not always be visible or measurable in the way personal development often is.

   Example: You could take a course on public speaking (personal development), but ER would involve understanding the emotional impact of your words, connecting authentically with your audience, and finding fulfillment in sharing your message.

4. **Personal Development Can Be Tactical; ER is Relational:**
   Personal development often involves concrete tactics and strategies, like setting goals, tracking progress, or building habits. ER is more relational, focusing on empathy, connection, and the emotional depth of your interactions

with others and yourself. It is about the quality of your relationships, both personally and spiritually.

Example: A leader may develop their strategic thinking through personal development, but ER would involve leading with compassion, understanding their team's emotional needs, and building trust.

The distinction between ER and personal development reminds me of two powerful truths found in these passages of the Bible:

"For what profit is it to a man if he gains the whole world, and loses his own soul? Or what will a man give in exchange for his soul?" Matthew 16:26: (NKJ)

It is a sober reminder that success, achievements, and wealth mean nothing if we lose the very essence of who we are—our soul, our purpose, our integrity, and our emotional richness. This verse challenges us to look beyond what the world dictates and ask ourselves what truly matters to us.

"Therefore, give to Your servant an understanding heart to judge Your people, that I may discern between good and evil. For who is able to judge this great people of Yours?" 1 Kings 3:7 (NKJ)

King Solomon took the throne of Israel as a child, but asked God for wisdom in ruling, so God gave him wisdom and gave him wealth! It is estimated that if King Solomon were alive today, his net worth would be approximately $2.2 trillion.

In the pursuit of success, wealth and ER, here are two questions to consider:

What areas of your life are successful but leave you feeling empty or disconnected?

What are you pursuing at the cost of your emotional, spiritual, or relational well-being?

Can Money Buy Happiness?

In a word, no, but it sure is a lot more fun to have money than not! This is a simple list of things money cannot buy. I am sure you can think of more.

1. Love
2. Trust
3. Happiness
4. Time
5. Health
6. Integrity
7. Wisdom
8. Friendship
9. Peace of Mind
10. Purpose
11. Gratitude
12. Empathy
13. Courage
14. Resilience
15. Character
16. Spirituality
17. Kindness
18. Fulfillment
19. Respect
20. Memories

Which of these resonates with you? Find your top five and use them as your guiding principles to begin building an emotionally rich life. Post them somewhere you will see them regularly to help you stay focused on what truly matters to you.

Success does not happen overnight, but the success you want, the kind that lasts and is effective, needs a firm foundation. In my opinion, character is shaped in the highs and lows of life and practicing ER is the fastest and most rewarding way to build our character and prepare for success.

Friends, I hope you found this insightful and helpful.

As always, I am cheering for you and wish you every success!

***

To contact Sharon:

Contact me at hello@sharonhughes.net

Connect on LinkedIn: https://www.linkedin.com/in/sharon-hughes-speaker/

Or visit my website: https://sharonhughes.net

I have a FREE gift for you, The Ultimate Guide To Discovering Your Leadership Voice planner. Request yours here: https://bit.ly/4eTPvI3

Trisha Fuller

Trisha Fuller is an award-winning Master Hypnotist & NLP Trainer/Practitioner and mentor.

International and TEDx Speaker, Co-Author of Amazon Best Seller

Trisha has been featured on iTunes and C-Suite Network, has spoken on stages at Oxford University and University Alberta, and facilitates workshops through The Canadian Hypnosis Academy.

Her active hypnosis clinics support thousands of clients in person and online. Trisha is passionate about helping others discover new techniques to balance family and career and support them with their goals: weight loss, stopping smoking, confidence, motivation, stress, and pain.

Lindsay's Story: A True Story, A Last Resort

By Trisha Fuller

Have you ever been so defeated that you didn't know what to do?

Do you struggle to remain composed and control your emotions?

Are you plagued with thoughts and memories that replay in your head?

That was Lindsay's life. She was desperate for a solution. After two years, she had finally hit rock bottom. With no hope left, she made an appointment. This appointment would transform her life.

Present Day

Lindsay stood at the window in her beautiful clinic, looking out. She felt a wave of gratitude come over her as she reflected on her journey. Her life had changed so much from her near-death experience years earlier to where she was now. Lindsay is a successful business owner, Consulting Hypnotist, and mother of two. Her journey seemed impossible, and she was astonished by how much she had accomplished over the last 7 years.

7 Years Earlier

Lindsay, 29, lay in the hospital. Eight doctors and nurses frantically tried to manage her care. Her pulse was extremely low, at 30 beats per minute. She could not hold up her arms. The left side of her body was completely numb, with no perception of hot and cold. Her ability to talk and swallow was gone. The simple act of breathing became a challenge. She could see her husband, Shane, tucked in the corner of the room, looking terrified. She thought it was the last time she would see him, and she was consumed by fear as her body was failing right before her eyes.

A CT had determined she was having a stroke; a neck manipulation had caused a bilateral tear of the vertebral artery, which had caused blood clots to form. She had received Tissue Plasminogen Activator (TPA), a clot-busting drug, and now she seemed worse than before. She felt like she was in a downward spiral with no end.

Lindsay returned to normal by some miracle and was released after 5 days in the Intensive Care Unit. For the following three weeks, she suffered from constant pain but was grateful to be alive.

Lindsay was continuing to heal day by day. One night, she got up from her bed, and her neck randomly cracked. It sent her into an instant panic attack, which has remarkably similar symptoms to a stroke. Lindsay woke her husband immediately, petrified that she needed to go to the hospital. Shane walked her through all the preventive tests. They determined she was not having a stroke, but the fear Lindsay had experienced remained.

In the years that followed, Lindsay was consumed with fear, panic, anxiety, and PTSD. She had tried multiple therapies, but nothing provided the solution she desperately needed.

The memory haunted her. She was grateful to be alive and thankful that she had recovered, but the event just kept playing on repeat in her mind. She could not sleep, felt anxious all the time, and her doctor kept pushing her to take antidepressants, which she did not believe was the solution to her issue.

Hugging people became a form of personal torture. She could no longer enjoy such a simple, caring act. Any action or pressure near her neck felt like a potential threat. Even moving her head too fast caused chaos in her nervous system. Life was a minefield, and she couldn't navigate her way through anymore.

Desperation set in. Overwhelming feelings and crying tormented her daily. Her husband and family could not help her, although they had tried. Guilt and shame set in, as she felt embarrassed that she couldn't solve this alone.

As a last resort, Lindsay sought out hypnosis. A few of her family members had recommended Trisha Fuller, as they had experienced personal success with hypnosis and neuro-linguistic programming (NLP). Lindsay thought it was ridiculous and doubted if it would work, but she was in such a bad place that she had to try something.

Lindsay made an appointment for a free hypnotic screening with Trisha. She knew she was in the right place after seeing hundreds of client stories posted around the office and videos showing success. The stories were of people just like her struggling to find their solution. She noticed that many people used hypnosis to lose weight, stop smoking, and boost confidence. The stories that resonated most with Lindsay were the ones involving people overcoming extreme stress, anxiousness, and fears. Seeing all the success stories made her feel less alone. Lindsay started to wonder if hypnosis and NLP might be her solution, too, and a spark of hope grew within her. However, there was still doubt. Could she do hypnosis and create her own success story?

As Lindsay turned to the last page of her paperwork, she froze. She needed to sign the waiver. The last time she signed a waiver, she ended up in the hospital. Could she trust anyone ever again? With racing thoughts, tears flooded her eyes and spilled down her cheeks, and she went into full panic mode. Trisha found her there, paralyzed with fear and unable to sign.

Lindsay slowly calmed down during her free screening and began to feel safer. She described to Trisha how fragile she felt, gripped in fear and struggling day to day. It was very curious that she was never asked to recount what had happened to her. Trisha only asked for a few bullet points rather than the whole story.

Trisha said, "A knowledge of content was not needed to facilitate change."

Lindsay was in awe. "Do you mean I don't have to talk about what happened over and over?" she replied.

"Do you focus in the rearview mirror when driving, or do you look forward and see the bigger view out the front window?" Trisha responded.

Lindsay paused, startled, then continued, "Forward, if you just look in the rearview mirror, you will crash."

"Exactly," Trisha replied. "The solution is in front of you. Your mind is not a video camera; when you replay the movie about what happened, the mind changes the memory. The memory is only a fragment of the truth. You delete, distort, and generalize it each time it is replayed. Many people get stuck in what happened. The solution requires a better question: what do you want, and what would your life look like, sound like, and feel like if you got exactly what you wanted out of this?"

Lindsay sat speechless.

"Lindsay, what do you want?" questioned Trisha.

"I don't want to cry. I don't want to feel like I can't leave the house…"

"Stop." Trisha put up her hand, cutting off Linday's statement. "I didn't ask you what you want to get rid of. I am asking what success looks like for you."

Lindsay took a deep breath and dared to hope momentarily, then said, "I want to sleep, feel calm, feel like I am in control, and stop the memory playing in my head."

"Ok, now we have something to work with! Stand up." Trisha insisted as she stood up as well. "What is the main thought that taunts you in your head?" she asked.

"Why did this happen to me?" Lindsay stated.

"Put your arms in the air and pretend like you are a little kid, kicking and screaming on the ground and yelling, 'Why did this happen to me?'" Trisha said. "Come on, I'll do it with you!"

Lindsay looked skeptically at Trisha and thought, *"What the heck is this lady wanting me to do?"* Finally, she raised her arms, threw them down, and yelled, "Why did this happen to me?!"

Trisha looked at Lindsay empathetically and stated, "That is you, having a temper tantrum every day. You want your way and are mad you don't have it."

Lindsay stood there intrigued. She listened carefully as Trisha explained four coping stances to help stop her temper tantrum, as outlined in Virginia Satir's book *The New People Making*.

The first stance was called the Blamer. Lindsay learned that it is when we point our mental finger and blame people, places, situations, and ourselves for various actions. It's demonstrated by pointing and saying, *"It's all your fault."*

The second coping stance was called the Placater. Lindsay was asked to put her hands before her face like she was talking to another human and say, *"I'll do anything for you. I am just here for you."* However, the Placater also has the Martyr within it, so Lindsay was then asked to say, *"I couldn't possibly take care of myself because I have all these people and things to take care of."*

Lindsay was then asked to cross her arms, look down her nose, and say, *"If one were to analyze this, one would find."* This was the third coping stance: the computer.

The fourth coping stance is the Distractor. She was told to kick her one foot out to the side, stick her thumb out like she was hitchhiking, stick her tongue out, and say squirrel. Then, go chasing after something sparkly. It was very peculiar but effectively demonstrated a person who could not stay on task.

Trisha finished her summary on the coping stances by stating, "We blame, placate, compute, and distract ourselves from success when we feel unsafe to level or surrender our previous position. This program will help you surrender your past position to feel safe and create your desired life."

"Lindsay, whose responsibility is it to change and create the life you want?" Trisha asked.

"Mine," Lindsay replied confidently.

With that simple realization, Lindsay began to believe she could move forward. It was pure magic for Lindsay. For the first time in a while, she stopped worrying about her past and became excited about the potential for her future.

During her free screening, Lindsay discovered that she could do hypnosis! She was amazed to learn that hypnosis is a brainwave state, which she had already experienced, like when she drove somewhere and didn't remember the last five minutes of the drive. She was relieved to learn that you don't black out during hypnosis and that she could stop it at any moment. She was in control since all hypnosis is self-hypnosis, a state of mind that achieves singular thought.

She was shocked to feel inspired but scared that her newfound optimism would disappear. She knew she had to do something. At once, she committed to taking action. She signed the waiver. She was done living a life she was not in control of and was ready to change.

Lindsay noticed a massive shift after her free screening and even more after the first session! It was like night and day. Her life had felt dark and secluded, and now it seemed brighter and more comfortable. She had no idea that hypnosis was so much fun! Lindsay didn't think change and recovery could be enjoyable, but this new mental shift made all the difference.

Lindsay loved that she also received hypnosis audios to utilize at home in between her sessions. She received a new one each week after her in-person session. She also could do hypnosis sessions online when she couldn't make it to the clinic. Her new hypnosis habits provided her with the calm that she needed, and each motivated her to begin taking action to shift her moods. She also learned that physical movements would change her state of mind, and being physically active helped her to calm herself.

One of the most effortless shifts she experienced was learning how to use water to let go of memories, negative thoughts, and even feelings! It was so quick and easy. She could drink water and *Wash Away* the unwanted! This fast, easy technique was reinforced in each session. It was instant magic for Lindsay! The best part was that she could utilize this technique anywhere! Trisha expanded *Wash Away* with *The Bomb* technique, a quick, easy NLP trick that helped Lindsay take the old memories, grab them, put them behind her, and make them explode like a bomb or fireworks. Then, she would wash it away with a drink of water while focusing on something she wanted in her life.

Skills and sessions focused on releasing memories, instant calming techniques, changing negative thinking, and forgiveness methods. Lindsay learned to utilize multiple NLP anchors, timeline techniques, and Ho'Oponopono.

By the end of her program, Lindsay had been taught how to do self-hypnosis. It was empowering to know that she could harness the power of her mind to work on anything that popped up in her daily life. She felt calmer, more in control, and more motivated in her personal and professional activities. She rarely thought about past events; they had lost their potency when they crossed her mind. She could now easily let these thoughts go and flip her thinking.

Lindsay recommended hypnosis and NLP sessions to several members of her family and friends, and they, too, began to do programs with Trisha. Lindsay was inspired by hypnosis, and she started training with Trisha to gain her certification in hypnosis and NLP.

Initially, Lindsay was afraid of being in a class and lacked confidence. However, the potential benefits of the course were far more important than her fear, so she pushed through. She knew Trisha would provide a safe learning environment, and her curiosity about helping others fueled her desire to continue.

Taking a hypnosis certification course was a pivotal moment for Lindsay. She fell in love with hypnosis. She felt inspired as she watched her fellow students transform their problems in just four days. The hypnosis training felt like a retreat. She worked on herself and learned hypnotic skills. She acquired an arsenal full of techniques and replaced her old models of relationship strategies and communication skills with more efficient ones.

Lindsay was astonished to discover that hypnotic language and neurolinguistics were utilized everywhere in media, advertising, and by public figures. By learning how these skills impact language and communication, she found she could effectively deliver her message to others and be better understood. She saw the most benefit in how she changed as a mother and wife. She felt more confident and could communicate calmly with her children and husband, which was a game changer for her.

Her husband, Shane, was so amazed at Lindsay's changes that he also took hypnosis training with Trisha.

Lindsay hadn't expected how much this course would affect her husband. After the training, he discovered that the hypnosis course helped him be a better husband, father, friend, and employee. It was amazing how a four-day course reduced his stress and gave him the control he needed to achieve even more professionally and personally, which was a happy side effect of the course. Shane was excited to learn the tools of the trade and began the certification process.

Lindsay and Shane completed their hypnosis certification through The Canadian Hypnosis Academy and Master Hypnotist Society. They were excited about the new opportunities that training provided them. They knew that the skills they learned were valuable in almost any career since hypnosis is a life skill. Hypnotic language is commonly used in teaching, advertising, medicine, politics, and most media and communication.

Many people don't realize that reoccurring thoughts are hypnotic. Lindsay wanted to be empowered by her thoughts, not controlled by them. She desired to help others find this control as well. She wanted them to have fun with the learning and to help others make changes quickly. She was inspired to create magic for them, just as she had magic created for her. Lindsay has found her purpose. She committed to life-long learning to fuel this passion.

NLP training with Trisha was just as transformational as hypnosis. They found it fascinating because it bypassed the critical faculty (conscious thinking barrier) of the mind so quickly. NLP was essentially waking hypnosis. It changed belief through the language patterns in the mind. If you just shifted where you pictured an old memory, the whole memory changed! And then, if you changed the sound and feeling associated with the memory, it became even less potent! This was only one technique in NLP. The potential for radical change was incredible!

Lindsay and Shane honed their skills by observing and working in Trisha's hypnosis clinic for their clinical practice. They mastered techniques and noticed that as they helped others change, they became more committed to their changes. Working with real clients made them more congruent in their actions, attitudes, and beliefs.

Within a few short months of becoming consulting hypnotists, Lindsay and Shane launched Calgary Hypnosis Solutions. Over the next few months, they knew they wanted more. They purchased the clinic Hypnosis for Health and Happiness from Trisha. Life was changing at a rapid pace for them, and they loved it!

Lindsay knew the importance of continued accountability and support. She signed up for personal and business mentorship with Trisha Fuller and Scott McFall, founder of the Master Hypnotist Society. Lindsay continued her education by taking more training with both Trisha and Scott. By continuing to learn, she expanded her skills and comfort zone. Lindsay found that committing to continued learning had a grounding effect on her. It helped keep her ego in check and focus on new solutions to help their clients. It also provided her with continued support. Lindsay knew her mentors were there to support her and were always available to assist if she had a question about a client or technique.

Lindsay valued that each training course focused on hands-on learning, which pushed her to learn by doing. She saw a technique, practiced, debriefed, and then repeated it.

Lindsay's journey was nothing short of amazing. She found the change she was looking for and took control of her life.

You, too, are capable of finding this change.

Are you ready to discover your solution?

Just like Linsday and Shane, you can discover fun and magical ways to facilitate change now. Don't wait. Take action now and get results faster and easier.

Lindsay and Shane are real people, just like you. They diminished the potency of old thoughts, emotions, and memories so they could be the architects of the life they craved. They discovered a passion for self-improvement through hypnosis and NLP, and you can too.

When you sign up for training with The Canadian Hypnosis Academy (www.LearnHypnosis.ca), you will get to experience and practice each method. This allows you to become a zealot, someone genuinely passionate about the art and science of hypnosis and NLP, ensuring a transformational experience.

***

To contact Trisha:

For more information on Trisha's work: www.LearnHypnosis.ca

call: 1-403-741-8669

email: HypnosisAB@gmail.com

Receive a free gift by emailing HypnosisAB@gmail.com and using the subject line: Free Gift from Cracking the Rich Code.

Marla Press

Marla Press, Founder of Speakers on Fire Academy, is a Public Speaking Coach, Life Coach, Art of Presence™ Trainer, international speaker, and best-selling author. She coaches you to wow every room, so you magnetically attract more clients and wealth.

Marla's mission is to help you speak so people listen. She shows you how to grab attention, build trust, engage your audience, and inspire action.

In her small-group programs and private coaching, Marla uses cutting-edge speaking techniques, her psychology degree, energy work, and targeted intuition. Whether you speak to one or to many, Marla's unique exercises help beginner and experienced speakers grow their business fast!

If you want to heat up your talk, ignite your compelling story, make your offers sizzle, fire up your cash flow, or you are ready to be "hot off The Press," Marla Press is your coach!

Invite Marla to speak at your event and she will get your audience fired up while demonstrating solutions to their challenges. Her talks include "Let's Get Engaged! 10 Ways to Engage Your Audience & Attract Clients and Wealth" and "The Art of Presence: Connections that Authentically Lead to Cash."

Marla has published 3 books on psychology in her Emotional Roller Coaster Series. Topics include finances, losing weight, and empty nesting.

Her book on speaking will be coming out soon.

Create the Richer You

By Marla Press, CEO of Speakers on Fire Academy

Zig, zag zig, zag, pivot, fall, get up, pivot, zig, zag, fall, get up, pivot. My success did not happen in a straight line or a line that was always going up. This is probably true for you, too.

The problem is that many people give up when the going gets rough. Find ways to cope with the down days and never ever give up on your dreams.

Here are the "Cliff Notes" to Cracking the Rich Code: Don't wait, know thyself, be thyself, hire a coach, live your passion, do the hard work, create win-wins, celebrate. Find a large Post-it-note, write down this list, and stick it on your computer. It's simple but not always easy.

Background:

In your business, as a speaker, and even with friends, you can resist telling the hard stories, but at some point, it is both cathartic and liberating to share them with others…and then let them go. It doesn't have to be a huge trauma, but, for you, it might be. So many people have overcome some sort of trauma either as a child or an adult. It could be a breakup, death in the family, drinking too much, or a business failure. For me, it was all of the above.

It started with my parents' divorce, being sexually abused as a little child and into my teenage years, the decision to drink too much in my 20's, choosing and staying in a respectable career for decades that was way beneath my abilities, my divorce due to my husband's depression and subsequent substance abuse, my two kids acting out and nearly destroying me, and then one after another within three months… my house almost burned down, my Mom died, then my Dad died. (As a side note, it's not unusual for couples in love to die soon after the other, but my parents divorced when I was 3 and lived at opposite ends of the country, and my dad wasn't even sick.)

Oh, there were lots of traumas, bad decisions, and failures in between, too many to just list here. And that's ok.

As I write this, I feel like you are sitting next to me, and I want to hear all about you. You have had some trauma, bad decisions, and disappointment in your life, too. It may be different than mine and to more or lesser degrees, but I know you feel it, too. And that's ok.

Keep reading if you want to hear the good stuff...

Through all that, I always found the good in people and the joy in parts of life.

There were lots of good parts. School came very easy to me. I graduated high school a year early and went to college to study psychology and philosophy. Every break I had, I traveled to Mexico, Europe, South America, and across the United States. Dancing and music gave me great joy, and I was constantly in musical plays and in a dance company.

Turning Point:

Creativity is the first thing that saved my life. Growing up I immersed myself in dance and theater, always being in musical plays and going to Broadway shows as often as possible. I learned modern dance, taught dance, and won awards for my choreography. Poetry flowed out of me as if it was the breath in my lungs.

Maybe, just maybe, this cultivation and connection with 'creating' allowed me to design my life in later years.

The second time my life needed saving was in my 20's. A friend turned me on to Lifespring. A lot of people thought it was a cult or mind re-programming. It was definitely not a cult, but it was mind re-programming in a good way.

It taught me that we get into patterns for security and to make ourselves right. It showed me that when you get out of your comfort zone, the greatest growth happens. It gave me the experience, through experiential exercises, of empowerment, acceptance, trust, leadership, and love.

The Art of Presence

The last piece that propelled me into the confident, successful woman I am today was studying The Art of Feminine Presence (now The Art of Feminine and Masculine Presence or just The Art of

Presence). There are 44 practices or experiential exercises that transformed the way I live my life.

Presence is often misunderstood. Most people think of it as the same as mindfulness…not thinking about the past or how what you are doing is going to affect the future but thinking about what is happening in the moment. Mindfulness is absolutely something we all need to practice.

Presence is taking it a step further. It is getting out of your cluttered, thinking, critical mind full of your to do list and all the stimuli coming in at that moment. I call this energy "head space." When you get out of your head space and into your full body energy, magic happens. You connect to the essence of who you are and a collective consciousness. You are more resourceful, more authentic, and more magnetic.

The Value of Experiential Exercises

In my masterclasses and coaching I take you through the experience of being in your full body energy. It does not come naturally to most people nor is it something you can explain intellectually. I invite you to connect with me to experience it. It only takes about 10 minutes, and it can be life changing.

I am a certified trainer in this art, and I am a certified Life Coach from this same school. In my speaking coaching, I use my psychology background and many of these experiential exercises to transform you into a magnetic, sought-after, successful speaker.

Most people don't learn by just getting information and they don't implement most of what they learn. Maybe you have seen that in yourself. These exercises, practices, and experiences transform you quickly and profoundly. That is why I am different as a speaking coach. It is so rewarding to see my clients transform so that their business and personal life get better.

Now, I absolutely love my life, and I tell myself that every day. I say, "I love my life" as I'm meeting interesting and inspirational people, zipping between Zoom meetings, speaking on live stages, hiking at the foothills of the Rocky Mountains, laughing with my amazing kids, and connecting with my loving friends.

What about you? How are you creating your life? Let's connect. I'd love to hear!

Lessons I Learned

Here are some of the lessons I learned. I hope they resonate with you and change your life in a big or small way. They are in no particular order, but you do have to read to the end to hear about the secret I didn't put in the "Cliff Notes."

DON'T WAIT

Don't wait til you think you are ready. You may never be completely ready.

Don't wait til your kids are grown. You will be a great role model for your kids.

Don't wait til you get more education whether it is from a university or youtube or wherever.

Don't wait til you have more money to invest. Spend money to make money.

Don't wait til you lose weight or feel you look the part. Be the part. Confidence is sexy.

BE YOURSELF

It is good to study successful people and do some of the strategies that got them there. It isn't good to try to be them. Be yourself.

Know who you are. You can take several tests to assess your personality. There are the typical ones, but there are also archetype ones and other unique angles. Explore several of them.

I also suggest lots of introspection. Ask yourself questions like what are you passionate about, what gives you joy, what are you good at, where do you want to be next year and in 5 years.

Don't try to hide what you don't like about yourself. Call it out. Say it out loud, then change it if you want.

Don't show up 2-dimentional. Be fully expressed with all your quirkiness and you will be much more interesting. I show my speaking clients how to do this all the time. It creates relatability and trust with your audience. It changes everything. Think of characters in a novel or movie. They are interesting because they are multi-dimensional with strengths and weaknesses and a unique combination of qualities.

INVEST IN YOURSELF

Invest in your self-care and your relationships.

Invest in your knowledge and skills.

Successful people take risks and believe they can make it work out.

Successful people invest money even when it is hard, because they know it will make them more money.

Invest in your business. Invest in a support team (of one or many) and other things you need to grow.

Invest in coaches. Good coaches show you how to do things smarter, more efficiently, and more effectively. You will grow faster.

FOLLOW YOUR PASSION

Know what your true passion is. It isn't always the first thing that comes to mind. Take your time asking yourself questions. Sit in a quiet place and trust what comes to you. Believe in your intuition.

Ok, I know from experience that just following your passion doesn't always pay. You have to do the hard work, stay dedicated in hard times, and stay focused.

Following your passion will help keep you motivated and bring you more joy.

Your dreams are about what is important to you. It includes your values and what you REALLY want, not what you think you should want.

CREATE WIN WINS

What are your beliefs about wealthy people or successful people?

Do you think everyone is your competition?

Do you think you have to step on others to get ahead?

These are just beliefs. Know your beliefs and what serves you best.

Create win wins or win win wins.

Learn from others, create good relationships, help others, collaborate, ask for support, and celebrate other people's wins.

CELEBRATE

Celebrate constantly.

Celebrate the small wins no matter how small.

Create significant rewards for yourself for the bigger wins.

Celebrate other people's wins…in your personal and business relationships.

Celebrate wins that have nothing to do with your work and ones that do.

THE BIG SECRET TO BIG FINANCIAL SUCCESS

Not everyone wants to work for themselves or make a million plus dollars, and that's ok.

If you want either, or both, of the above, create your own business.

Create your own business and become an exceptional speaker.

Speakers are some of the highest paid people in the world.

You can't just be good; you have to get results.

That includes having a message that people want to hear, creating a personal brand, being able to grab and keep attention, telling compelling stories, entertaining, connecting, building trust, inspiring action, and knowing the strategies to build a successful business around speaking.

You Are Probably Asking:

You're probably asking, "Marla, why didn't you write your whole chapter around all those skills you just mentioned above?"

That's because I can tell you how to have the mindset and general strategy to find success and wealth, but I can't tell you how to be a great speaker. I have to take you through exercises and the experience of communication that can truly wow the room. Then you must practice it and get feedback. I get you out of your mind, and into your full presence and energy.

It is then that your speaking goes from pretty good to exceptional. You draw people in, and they want more. You no longer have to chase speaking gigs, because you are a sought-after speaker.

Let's Get Engaged!

Titles are important, and this is one of my talk titles which always gets a reaction. It is also the biggest key to your success. No matter how good your message is or how great your teaching points are, if you don't engage your audience, you won't inspire action. This is true if you are talking on a big stage, to one potential client, to your partner, or to your kids. It is especially true if you want to speak on any stage.

The old ways of speaking no longer work. People don't want tons of information; they want connection and an experience. They can get information everywhere. Yes, you want to give valuable teaching points and actionable steps, but when you engage your audience, they want to have more of you. When you engage your audience, they are motivated to take action. They also remember what you told them and especially how you made them feel. When they feel something, they are inspired to take action.

Here Are 10 Ways to Engage an Audience:

1). Hook them immediately—with humor or an unusual statistic or something unexpected

2). Tell compelling stories—start in the middle of the action, paint word pictures, make it about them

3). Use humor often—you don't have to tell jokes. Find the humor in everyday happenings everyone can relate to.

4). Body language—don't just stand or sit there and don't pace. Make your body language emphasize your points. Move with intention. Be congruent with your words because it will build trust. This includes facial expressions which is especially important on Zoom.

5). Use technology—if you are going to use slides, have emotional images and few words. If you are online, there are so many ways to create interest with tech. Use video, OBS studio, etc.

6). Use props—Not always necessary, but when used in congruence with your message, it adds interests, humor, and engagement. I use rubber chickens when talking about people feeling chicken about doing videos or being on stage. People love to squeeze my chickens and hear the funny sounds.

7). Signature move or sound—creating a signature move or sound will create anticipation and engage your audience both from speech to speech and within the same talk.

8). Movement—get your audience to move. Either stand up or a thumbs up or raise their hand. Don't ask for the same movement over and over like raising hands. Vary it. Sometimes I ask people to hold out their hand and I make the suggestion I am putting something in it. There are lots of ways to encourage movement. When people move physically, they are more likely to move mentally and emotionally, too.

9). Do an activity—the length of your talk will dictate the type of activity. It could be as simple as saying look to your right and high five the person next to you or it could be taking your audience through a visualization or quick breathwork or breakout session.

10). Be fully present—when you practice and condition yourself to be in your full body presence, you will be authentic and magnetic. You will reach people on a deep level, and they will not only connect with you, but hear your message more clearly. There is so much to being fully present. Set up a time with me or come to a masterclass and I will show you how.

You can come up with more ideas for these techniques on your own, and I hope these ideas have really sparked your creativity. The next step for you will be to practice and get feedback from someone who has been in the speaking world a long time. You might want a coach to give you more ideas and the experience of taking your speaking to the next level. It is then that you will wow the room and magnetically and authentically attract more clients and wealth.

You will create the "Richer You." There are so many kinds of riches in this life. Not everyone has the same needs or goals. You will attract abundance, as much financial wealth as you desire, interesting and supportive people all around, a joyful and fulfilling lifestyle, and all the tangible and intangible riches you can imagine.

Let's get started!

To contact Marla:

Schedule a Hot or Not Speaker Eval or a Get to Know You Session http://speakwithmarla.com

Reserve a spot for the next free masterclass https://bit.ly/speakers-masterclass

Connect on Linkedin https://linkedin.com/in/marlaapress

Check out Marla's website https://marlapress.com

Email Marla m.press@marlapress.com

Download Marla's Speakers on Fire Academy App https://bit.ly/MarlaPressApp

Choose how you want to connect or what info you want https://linktr.ee/MarlaPress

Chase Hughes

Chase Hughes is CEO of Applied Behavior Research and #1 bestselling author of five books on influence and behavior skills.

Chase develops and teaches advanced skills in persuasion, influence, interrogation, and behavior profiling. Referred to by Entrepreneur Magazine as the 'Jason Bourne of psychology,' Chase teaches not only the public, but elite intelligence agencies around the world. He was named with Mark Zuckerberg in the top 40-under-40 CEO's of the year, and was called the 'best of the best' by Dr. Phil.

After 20 years of service in the US military, Chase developed the '6MX behavior profiling system for intelligence agencies, now known as the gold standard in tradecraft. Chase is also a trial consultant, assisting in jury selection and courtroom strategy. He's the *only* trial consultant in the world to offer a 300% money-back guarantee.

Chase is also the creator of the PEACE-4A system for police de-escalation, and violence-prediction to save both the lives of officers and the public.

Chase focuses his time now on teaching behavior skills to the public, and enhancing the way we all connect, communicate, and influence the world around us. Chase's company motto reflects all that he does in business: 'We rise by lifting others.'

Your New Butler

By Chase Hughes

By the time you read this, you've already become someone new.

Almost every problem in our lives comes from a *single* source, and all of our success comes from the *same* source: Time-traveling priorities. I promise I'll unpack this in a sec...

Lots of people tell you they have the secret to success; some will tell you they will change your life. This chapter will.

Imagine waking up in a pristine bedroom. You feel amazing as you sit up in bed and see that your clothes have been laid out for you. Even your shoes are in the perfect spot; laid out so that you need minimal effort to put them on.

When you go downstairs, the coffee or tea is already set up, and your kitchen is clean and welcoming. The stuff you need for work is laid out near the door as you exit. All your to-do lists, books you need, and the phone charger that you've been promising yourself you'd bring to work one day – it's all laid out for you. As you climb into your car, you see that it's full of gas.

You deserve this. You've lived long enough without it.

One more scenario:

Imagine that for the past six months, you've been enjoying the lavish benefits of having a butler. Your butler has been taking good care of you; setting everything you need up for you, and even forcing you to eat the right food. The butler even paid all your bills on time, kept in touch with old friends, and helped you get those Christmas cards all sent out. They did everything just for you. What would your life look like? What would YOU look like?

How many times have you woken up late for something because you stayed up too late the night before? How many hundreds of decisions left you pissed off at your past-tense self?

Most of our life's issues stem from this single failure: putting the needs of your present-tense self above your future-self. We might think something like, 'I can stay up all night…I'll figure it out tomorrow.'

YOU AREN'T THE PROBLEM, BUT YOU USED TO BE

People do stupid things. I'm no exception.

I hear it from clients all the time:

- I need to lose weight
- I have no discipline
- I'm massively in debt
- I can't get it all done
- I'm overwhelmed
- I can't get to the gym
- I can't lose weight
- Somehow, I can't stop smoking
- I can't stop overeating
- I can't stop losing my cool with people at work
- I'm always late
- I never have things planned well

These are only a few. Chances are you've uttered similar statements. There are books and training courses for all these things. 'How to Get Organized,' 'How to lose weight super-fast,' 'how to have self-discipline.' They all have a technique that worked for **some** people…sometimes.

There's a shocking secret I'd like to share with you; all those problems above stem from the *exact* same issue.

Would a butler be able to help you with lots of these things? All of them, perhaps? Absolutely!

Here's the major issue:

Your *current* behavior is not the problem. Your *past* behavior is.

Let me unpack this and show you how it's true:

Over the course of your life, you've accumulated a lot of habits. The problems never came from a choice to smoke, drink too much, stay up too late, ignore the teachers in school, or eat an entire bag of Cheetos.

Our issues stem from one central thinking pattern: a failure to prioritize the benefits of your *future self*. Our success or failure is a result of how much priority we assign to our future self *over* our present self. All the decisions we regret have their roots in this lack of future self-prioritization.

The past-tense 'you' didn't give a sh*t about the present-tense 'you.' They only cared for themselves. After twenty years of study in human behavior, success, influence, and persuasion, I discovered that successful people do a lot of things. People tend to analyze what they do in the present instead of what they did in the past, to become successful. They may have common habits or morning routines we can spend weeks dissecting and analyzing, but there's one thing they all have in common that got them to where they are now:

They all prioritized their future-self over their present-self. Let me show you a few examples:

1. A world-leading surgeon applied to college; his friends wanted to party instead while he went to classes he didn't even enjoy.
2. A champion boxer who's called an 'overnight success' decided to train daily for twenty years while his friends chose to use drugs or 'relax.'
3. A 75-year-old man who's in amazing shape spent a lifetime eating nutritious foods and exercising attends the funeral of a friend who ate like a king.
4. The successful CEO, for decades, opted out when his friends would skip class, miss work, or collect unemployment because it was easy.

Look at anyone who's successful; you'll find this quality. Their lives are a product of foregoing present-tense gratification in favor of *future enjoyment* and benefit. In an ideal world, the person who has lived with this butler in their lives feels three things throughout their day:

1. Gratitude for the decisions of their ***past***-self.
2. Discipline toward the ***present***-tense self.
3. Deep concern for the welfare of their ***future***-self.

We've been pissed off at our past-tense self, way too often. We stayed up too late when there was an exam or a big meeting the next day. We ate a plate-full of crap when we knew we'd regret it. We drank too much at a party knowing our future-self would suffer. We decided to head out with friends instead of finishing that task from work; letting our future-self bear the burden of punishment.

> This shows up in every aspect of your life no matter who you are. Your future-self deserves better, and your present-self deserves a freaking butler. Life's about to change.

QUIET ENJOYMENT

We all know these people; they are the friends we had in high school who showed up late to the party because they were finishing an English paper. They always had the clean bedroom growing up that we secretly envied. They cancelled plans because a task came up that you thought was ridiculous considering how boring and trivial it was. Who says no to a night out for something like cleaning out a closet? Seriously?

The single *present-tense* quality that successful people all share is 'quiet enjoyment.' This (seemingly) innate ability to calmly get things done that other people would put off, neglect, or ignore.

We imagine them happily sifting through thousands of pages at their kitchen table to get their taxes done, or whistling gleefully as they fold their laundry, placing it neatly into their drawers as little birds fly around the house like in a Disney movie.

This isn't the case.

While they are sitting there at the kitchen table, or placing that folded shirt into their drawer, it's not a scene from a musical. Often, they are **not** enjoying the moment. In reality, they are *quietly enjoying* something else as these tasks are getting completed. Their butler completes this task for them while they are focused on the future; the benefit they will get from doing this, or the moment itself. It's not the *task* that brings them enjoyment, it's the *benefit*, the act of doing it, the sheer completion of it.

If you look through your yearbook and find that popular kid who also managed to get into Yale somehow, you'll probably remember that they had this quality. They had Quiet Enjoyment running in the background of all their mental programs. They still showed up to the parties, but *after* they completed their tasks at home (which we didn't see). They still socialized and got into mischief, but quietly, in the background, they completed things that others didn't.

These people can quietly enjoy doing things that others put off or ignore.

We're going to bring this into your life, and it's going to be kickass. The benefit that you'll have over these other people is that your butler is going to be doing all these things for you. The butler will focus on the future, not the moment.

Would a complete devotion to the welfare of a future-self have stopped someone from smoking, drinking too much, staying out too late, spending too much money? You bet. The issue is that so many 'coaches' address the symptoms of this problem, instead of the cause. It all goes back to prioritizing your future self.

When you absolutely crush this (and you will!), it has a snowball effect that will make it incredibly addictive.

Success is a result of tiny tasks, quietly completed, that others choose not to do.

Discipline is the ability to prioritize the needs of your future-self over your own.

Be your own butler.

WHAT NO ONE TALKS ABOUT

Social media has given us a lot. But we tend to only see the top 1% of people's lives; assuming that all these other people are perfect, living in flawless houses and never having bad days.

When we see people who go to the gym every day, it's admirable. You might think to yourself, 'Wow. I wish I had that level of discipline!'

The truth is that you *do*. And here's the secret that none of them will tell you. **What you're seeing there is not discipline, it's habit.** These people only needed about a teaspoon of discipline to start going to the gym regularly. After a few days, it became a habit. This 'magic' ability they possess to eat healthy, work out, and stay in great shape is all habit formed with a few drops of discipline.

Discipline is an expendable resource. Think of discipline like a hundred bucks. Every day, you get a hundred dollars when you wake up. Having to pick out clothes, decide what to eat, make coffee, check the gas tank, and force yourself to go for that quick run on your lunch break, all costs money. Each one costs a lot at first.

Let's assume each task costs twenty dollars. Picking out clothes, deciding what to eat, making coffee, struggling to find your car keys, rushing to add gas to your tank...these would quickly burn through that hundred bucks. By the time lunch rolls around, the break room with free bags of chips might seem a lot more tempting than going for a run and having to shower.

When we start new habits, it costs more. The more often they are *repeated*, the less they cost. They move gradually from requiring discipline to 'just part of the day.'

When you make a list of new-year's resolutions a mile long, what happens? It takes too much discipline to do them all at once. This 'money' is spent, so trying to 'fund' all these new activities it's easy to burn out.

What would all this mean in a summarized list?

- You only need a little discipline to start and form a habit
- The more you set your future-self up for success, the more discipline you have the following day
- The repetition of these life-changing tasks diminishes the effort required to complete them over time

MAKING IT ALL WORK

If you met yourself in 30 years, would they be upset with you, or would they hug you and thank you? What habits would you plead with your younger self to adopt or *drop*?

The more you're able to prioritize the welfare of your future-self, the more you will be focused on them. I want you to care for your future self like they are the most important person in your life, because they are!

Implement a system to force yourself to think of your future self. Here's a one-month breakdown of how you could bring all of this into your life:

Week 1:

Download one of those apps that makes you look 40 years older. Print a few photos of your older self and put them where they will be relevant and keep you 'thinking forward.' For instance, you might place them on the fridge, the desk, in the car, or anywhere else they will impact your judgment in the moment. This will get your brain to start rewiring itself – focusing its awareness away from you and onto the 'you' in the future.

Week 2:

Start doing little favors for future-you! Before you go to bed, get the coffee ready for them. As you enter your bedroom at night, set out an outfit for them. I want you to say to yourself (out loud) 'They will love this!' Make dinner ahead of time, order your future self a gift that won't arrive immediately. These small acts will reprogram your brain a little more – getting it to tie future thinking with reward and enjoyment.

Week 3:

Continue putting things in your life that make you future focused. This reward process you're setting up will become addictive very soon. You're now into the 21-day mark! That (according to some people) means you're in HABIT territory! This week do a few things that are a little further in the future. Think of things that your future-self will absolutely love. You could open a savings account that is hidden from sight for them to find later, like a little money time capsule. You could set a few calendar reminders on your phone for way in the future to congratulate yourself or remind them that you were thinking of them way back then (now). Get creative. They (you) will thank you.

Week 4:

Make a two-part list of what you'd like in the future:

Part one: The daily activities and tasks that you will perform for your future self. Like setting up coffee, building to-do lists for the following day, or making sure there's plenty of healthy food ready to go for tomorrow's 'you.'

Part two: The one-year list. What would you need to start doing now to 'build' the ideal you, and the ideal life for you? Leave a sticky note where you will find it later in the future that simply says, 'I was thinking of you.'

What would happen in a year if you only worked for the welfare of future you? How would your life look? How would your health, finances, relationships, and even happiness change? It took me twenty years to discover this single method to fast-track success. I want you to have in in twenty minutes.

Holly: Past self does not define you – helped you become you – today's self can help you for future

Whatever your past-self did, forgive them. It's no longer *you*. Until you feel massive gratitude for your past-self setting you up for enjoyment and success, send them forgiveness. Your new way of life is to **take care of that person you will never meet but will always be contributing to**:

future-you.

You absolutely can do this. Not only do you deserve it, just imagine how thankful and proud the future you will be. One more time; you *can* do this!

***

To contact Chase

Chase's website: www.ChaseHughes.com

Cindy MacCullough

Cindy MacCullough is a passionate life coach, entrepreneur, and strategist with over 25 years of corporate leadership experience. As the founder of **Life Pivot**, she helps individuals tackle life's biggest transitions—career shifts, personal reinventions, and everything in between. A Master Certified Life Coach, Cindy combines real-world business savvy with deep personal insights to empower clients to overcome fear, build confidence, and create bold, purpose-driven lives.

Drawing from her extensive career leading high-growth strategies and transformational initiatives for startups and global organizations, Cindy knows how to turn challenges into opportunities. She's built high-performing teams, spearheaded multimillion-dollar ventures, and mastered the art of navigating change, both professionally and personally. Her own journey through major life pivots fuels her passion for helping others do the same.

Cindy's coaching philosophy is rooted in action, resilience, and self-discovery. She equips clients with practical tools to break free from fear, redefine their path, and thrive in ways they never thought possible. Her empathetic yet strategic approach inspires individuals to embrace uncertainty and move forward with clarity and power.

Her mission? To turn life's toughest pivots into unstoppable momentum. Whether you're stuck, scared, or simply ready for more, Cindy's expertise and energy will help you create the life you've always envisioned—bold, impactful, and entirely yours.

When the Rubber Meets the Road

By Cindy MacCullough

Let's go! Sounds simple, right? What if you don't know how to get started? What if you aren't clear on where you are going? Even worse, what if you are experiencing fear and doubt at every turn?

Although I've heard the saying a thousand times before, it never resonated with me like it did the other day. Maybe it's because, on this occasion, I was deeply reflecting on big changes happening in my own life—impending changes that could impact my cash flow and financial security.

"When the rubber meets the road" is the perfect metaphor for moments in life where big decisions are looming. It's the moment of truth. The moment when you show up or give up. For a competitive runner, it's when the pistol fires and the laps start. Would their tireless hours of training pay off? Would they finish their day with a spot on the winner's podium? It can be the moment when a relationship is at that final cusp, and the partners decide to resolve their issues or go their separate ways. Or the moment when a career just doesn't fit anymore. Does a burnt-out employee give up a stressful, high-paying career to risk it all on their dream job? Each of us faces these pivotal moments in our lives. Sometimes we win, sometimes we fail, and sometimes we never even try.

Having experienced numerous big career changes, health challenges for loved ones around me, and the graceful end of a ten-year marriage, I've experienced all the facets of making substantial life pivot decisions. I've also had the honor of supporting many others through these very personal and critical times.

In reading this chapter, identify the main area of your life where the rubber meets the road. The ideas below can be applied to any personal or professional situation. Let's go exploring…

The BRAKES

A straight stretch, no cars in sight, a full tank of gas, treats for the way, destination plugged into the GPS. And yet, you are at a standstill. No movement—just the full-on force of friction from the pavement and the deep press on the brakes preventing acceleration.

While the intention and route exist, there are forces preventing a successful journey or even the initial turn of the key. This debilitating force is typically its strongest when considering venturing into the unknown or pushing into new and challenging situations. Our brakes are the thoughts and emotions that prevent us from reaching our destination: fear, guilt, limiting beliefs or imposter syndrome are a few of the most common. Your brakes can stop you from ever leaving the driveway—or even getting into the car to start with. Standing staring from the porch, paralyzed with keys firmly clenched in the palm of your hand. Let's consider some factors that may present as little roadblocks or full-on barriers on your journey.

Fear is a powerful force, often rooted in the fear of failure, change, judgment, or even success. It feels real and can be downright paralyzing. Those gripped by fear frequently seek out evidence to justify and reinforce it, falling into a cycle of excuses that keeps them stuck. They cling to the comfort of the "known," forgetting that change is the only constant in life.

Excuses become a shield against the unknown: "It's cloudy, it might rain"; "It's late, I'll leave tomorrow." These justifications make it easy to delay action, but the cost is progress and growth. To break free, we must recognize fear for what it is—a hurdle, not a roadblock—and choose to step into the unknown, where transformation truly begins.

"F-E-A-R has two meanings: 'Forget Everything and Run' or 'Face Everything and Rise.'" ~ Zig Ziglar. What will you choose to do?

An all-or-nothing mindset can be a significant brake, holding us back from progress. Many of us believe that if we can't get it perfect on the first try, it's best not to try at all. This rigid, black-and-white thinking creates a false "either-or" narrative, leaving no room for growth or discovery. In reality, both perspectives can be true at the same time. The most valuable lessons often emerge from the grey zone—where missteps, compromise, and persistence come together.

Imagine taking a corner too fast, overcorrecting slightly but staying on the road. The next time you approach similar signs, you navigate with greater caution and confidence. By allowing ourselves the grace to step into new experiences, even imperfectly, we open the door to learning, growth, and eventual mastery—far more rewarding than avoiding the challenge altogether.

Guilt often acts as a heavy brake, slowing us down and keeping us from moving forward. Many of us become so consumed with carrying the burdens, worries, and happiness of others that we neglect our own "vehicle" and path. Too often, we step aside—delaying or even abandoning our journey—to let others take the wheel, convinced they are more deserving, even when we've cleared the way through our own effort. This misguided belief that prioritizing ourselves takes away from others only holds us back. In truth, ensuring our well-being isn't selfish—it's essential. Keeping our own "vehicle" in top condition makes us better equipped to support and care for those we love. Claiming and maintaining your lane is vital to becoming the best version of yourself.

Limiting beliefs like "I'm not good enough," "I'm not smart enough," and "Good things don't happen to me" typically stem from deep and long-rooted patterns. They might be why you never visit some cities or take different routes. This tendency to assume certain things are true will limit the routes you take and the things you allow yourself to experience. It is especially important to see these belief patterns and ask yourself: "Is it true?" Is it really true that if I take Route 46, I will be stuck in traffic, that I risk being carjacked, or that I will get a flat tire? Asking if it's true could be followed by, "Why do I believe this to be true? When did I first experience this belief?

Imposter syndrome. This one is my personal favorite and the one that most often keeps me in the driveway. "I'm no Porsche, so how can I win the race? I'm an older manual model, and the new model is so much sleeker. Everyone will see that I'm outdated".

Self-judgment is not our ally here, friends. We find countless reasons to believe we are not good or experienced enough to be in the position or role we have earned because others see our value. A step back is in order to allow ourselves to see what others do and to understand that our perspective is the unique combination of our life experiences—no other person is the same or can match that in any way. Take a moment to reflect on those big experiences, what you have learned, and carry them forward with you. Like the worn luggage with a zipper that sometimes snags — you have earned the role of being the favorite and trusted travel bag.

These and many other factors can keep us stopped and stagnant even when we know where we want to go. Recognizing your brakes will likely come into play at some point—the first step is to ease off them. Ask yourself:

- What is keeping me from moving forward?
- What are my fears and judgments surrounding the change?
- Now that I see these brakes, how can I change my perspective to move forward?

Overcoming the brakes is the only way you grow, evolve, experience new things, and catapult yourself to new heights. The real reward comes when you dig deep and not only identify the reasons "why to" move but also find the gas and go. You may discover that the scenery is amazing, you will meet new people along the way, and you will find a great restaurant with the most incredible cheesecake.

Remember: "When you change the way you look at things, the things you look at change." ~ Albert Einstein

The GAS

When in life do you get in the car and just start driving with no destination in mind? You typically have a purpose—a clear goal in mind—before you even get behind the wheel. You might be running an errand, driving the kids to sports or school, heading into work, or going to visit a friend at a fun social event. In all cases, you are dressed for the occasion, have all the items you need, and most often, you have also charted the most efficient route. The same should hold true when embarking on a big life change.

Define your North Star. Above all, the "why" of your life's pivot moment must be clear and motivating enough to keep you on track. Are you seeking freedom, growth, security, or fulfilling your life purpose? Being crystal clear about your "why" is the turbo charge to your engine and will be the reason you move swiftly and in the right direction. The "why" will always be your North Star—guiding and directing you.

Set your compass. What is the direction you need to take? Figure out what steps need to happen between where you are now and where you want to be. Define what success looks like when you reach your destination. Is it a new job? A new partner? Being happy single? What is the destination, and what are the key milestones along the way? Write these down, chart your course, and document your progress.

Be responsible. I don't mean "don't drink and drive". However, that is also a good rule of thumb. This is your life, and it will be the result of the decisions and actions that you take. You may struggle at times to keep the momentum going, but one thing is certain: if you never try, you will never succeed. Ultimate growth and success come when you move outside your comfort zone. While others can be there to lend support and guidance, you are solely in the driver's seat. You owe it to yourself to make the most of this life—it's your responsibility to do so.

Simply put: "You miss 100% of the shots you don't take." ~ Wayne Gretzky

Set your timeline. A rough idea of your journey's timeline will ensure that you stay on track and don't deviate for too long in any aspect. It's very easy to get distracted if you aren't clear on where you are going and your desired arrival time. Imagine if you ran out of money halfway through your journey because you stopped at too many fast-food restaurants! Checking how far you are from your destination at regular intervals will also encourage you to reassess your priorities and pivot if needed.

Fill your tank. This often-overlooked practice is essential to maintaining energy and focus. Just as a car cannot run on empty, neither can we. Recharging isn't selfish; it's an investment in your goals and well-being. Whether it's a quiet cup of coffee, a short walk, or reading something you enjoy, these small acts of self-care fuel your resilience, creativity, and ability to handle life's challenges with clarity. Ask yourself: What truly recharges me? Identify those activities and make them a non-negotiable in your daily routine.

Take action. We all have a multitude of great ideas, but unless we write them, speak them, or act on them, the ideas are unmaterialized and have no impact. In reality, unactioned ideas may be the biggest source of frustration for those of us who want to make a difference in the world but, due to the brakes above, never push forward. *Consistency in action is the key.*

Clarity surrounding our journey's where, when, how, and most importantly why is fundamental. You would not leave for a road trip without these basics—contemplate them deeply and spend the time you need to define your course, actions, and milestones. Hold yourself lovingly accountable along the way. Ask yourself:

- Why am I making this change?
- What will it mean when I get there?
- What will it mean if I don't?

The ROAD

Navigate. You will be faced with twists and turns along the way. Seldom do things happen exactly as you plan. Success can also be measured by how well you navigate a change in course and the twists and turns that present. Plans may need to be course-corrected as new information comes to light or as a result of a single decision. When this happens, the brakes will no doubt engage somewhat or fully. See it for what it is. Slow down but remember to once again engage the gas and stay the course to reach your destination.

Fork in the road. It is essential to remember that you always have choices. Sometimes, it's hard to remember this or believe it is true. At a minimum, your reaction to any given twist or turn is a choice. When the brakes engage, how will you respond? Will you come to a complete stop or see it for what it is, slow down, course-correct, and reengage the gas? The most challenging and defining moments in our lives are when things don't go according to our plan, and we suffer negative consequences. How we recover will define how and if we reach our destination.

"The best-laid plans of mice and men often go astray." ~ Robert Burns.

You will face twists and turns in your plans, and you will be faced with unforeseen choices along the path of any worthwhile destination. When this happens, take a pause and ask yourself:

- What choices do I have?
- How do I react when things don't go my way?
- How might I respond in a different way?

The DESTINATION

You've worked hard, and you've arrived. You hit the brakes, maybe even slammed on them a few times. You saw them, worked through them, and pressed the gas through the twists and turns, choosing a direction at every fork in the road. Maybe the journey was smooth, or maybe there were some potholes or even a flat tire along the way. And still... you've arrived, and it's time to get out of the car! Take a big stretch, grab a beverage, and relax.

Celebrate. When we reach the destination, we often rush onto the next big idea. We don't pause to celebrate or even acknowledge making it through the journey. We are already complacent at this win, thinking, "I'm not happy now; I'll be happy when...". Take a moment to celebrate reaching your destination.

Reflect. What did you learn along your journey? What made you hit the brakes, and what inspired you to press the gas? How did you navigate the twists and turns? Each experience offers valuable lessons that shape how you approach future challenges. Take time to consciously acknowledge these insights—they are the building blocks of growth and the key to navigating the road ahead with greater confidence and wisdom.

Thank. All life changes, big and small, are a journey. Whether you realize it or not, you went through all of the experiences described above. Take a moment to show gratitude for all the stops along the way. The convenience store attendant who made you smile while you were annoyed by the price of gas. The apple pie from the small diner that crumbled on your lap but delighted your taste buds. The stranger who stopped to help you with a flat tire. Take a moment to thank the people, challenges, and choices you made along the way to make it to your destination.

You've reached your destination and may already be packing for the next journey. Before you go, ask yourself:

- What did I learn?
- How did this journey impact my future?
- How will I celebrate and give thanks?

"Do not go where the path may lead, go instead where there is no path and leave a trail." ~ Ralph Waldo Emerson

When the Rubber Meets the Road Worksheet

Step 1: Identify Your Starting Point

- Where are you now?
- Reflect on your current situation.
- What area of your life feels stuck?
- Examples: Career, relationship, personal growth, health.

My current situation is:

_____
_____
_____
_____

What's stopping you?

Identify your "brakes" (fears, doubts, or limiting beliefs).

The Brakes Holding Me Back Are:

_____
_____
_____

Step 2: Define Your Destination

What do you want to achieve?

Describe your goal. Be as specific as possible.

My destination is:

_____
_____
_____
_____
_____

Why is this important?

What will achieving this goal mean to you?

My North Star (My Why) Is:

_____
_____
_____

Step 3: Plan Your Journey

Chart Your Course

Write down key milestones or steps needed to achieve your goal.

Examples: Update your resume, schedule time for self-care, or have a difficult conversation.

My milestones are:

Set a Timeline

Assign deadlines to your milestones.

My Timeline:

Step 1: _____ (Deadline: _____)

Step 2: _____ (Deadline: _____)

Step 3: _____ (Deadline: _____)

Step 4: Recognize Your Brakes

What fears or doubts are coming up?

My fears are:

How can I challenge these fears?

Reframe My Fear into a Positive Action:

___

Step 5: Fuel Your Tank

What brings you joy or recharges you?

List activities that energize you and commit to doing them regularly.

My refueling activities are:

___

How will you celebrate small wins along the way?

Reward ideas for milestones:

___

Step 6: Overcome Obstacles

What will you do when you encounter a setback?

Write down strategies to stay on course.

My strategies for navigating twists and turns are:

Who can you lean on for support?

List mentors, friends, or resources that can help.

My support system Includes:

_____
_____
_____
_____

Step 7: Reflect and Celebrate

What have you learned during the journey?

Lessons I've learned are:

_____
_____
_____
_____

How will you celebrate reaching your destination?

My celebration plan is:

_____
_____
_____
_____

Final Thoughts

Ask yourself these key questions:
- Why am I making this change?
- What will it mean when I achieve my goal?
- What will it mean if I don't?

Reflections:

_____
_____
_____
_____

To contact Cindy:

For more content, self-development tools, or to explore life coaching contact:

cindy@lifepivot.com

www.lifepivot.com

613.794.2876

Afterword

Life and business are always a series of transitions... people, places, and things that shape who we are as individuals. Often, you never know that the next catalyst for improving your business and life is around the corner, in the next person you meet, next mentor you listen to or the next book you read.

Jim Britt has spent over four decades influencing individuals and entrepreneurs with strategies to grow their business, developing the right mindset and mental toughness to thrive in today's business environment and to live a better life overall. Allowing all you have read in this book to create a new you, to reinvent yourself and your business model if required, because every business and life level requires a different you. It is your journey to craft.

Cracking the Rich Code is a series that offers much more than a book. It is a community of like-minded influencers from around the world. A global movement. Each chapter is like opening a surprise gift, that just may contain the one idea that changes everything for you. Watch for future releases and add them to your collection.

The work of Jim Britt has filled seminar rooms to maximum capacity and created a worldwide demand. If you get the opportunity to attend one of his live events, jump at the chance. You'll be glad you did.

Become a coauthor: If you are a coach, speaker, consultant of entrepreneur and would like to get the details about becoming a coauthor in the next Cracking the Rich Code book in the series, contact Jim britt at: support@jimbritt.com

STRUGGLING WITH MONEY ISSUES?

Check out Jim's latest program "Cracking the Rich Code" which focuses on the subconscious programs influencing one's financial success, that keeps most living a life of mediocrity. This powerful four-month program is designed to change one's relationship with money and reset your money programming to that of the wealthy. More details at: www.CrackingTheRichCode.com

To Schedule Jim Britt as a featured speaker at your next convention or special event, online or live, email: support@jimbritt.com

Master each moment as they become hours that become days.

Make it a great life!

Your legacy awaits.

STAY IN TOUCH

www.JimBritt.com

www.JimBrittCoaching.com

www.CrackingTheRichCode.com

www.PowerOfLettingGo.com for 2 FREE audios

www.JimBrittAcademy.com